Praise fo

"Howard Breen has written a wonderful book in ***The Toothpick Factory*** to guide young people. His lessons in life will help you succeed. Be sure to work through the personal branding exercise. I wish I had this resource 30 years ago..."

-Bob Leonidas, President/CEO Nestle Canada

"***The Toothpick Factory*** Howard Breen gives practical advice for any age on how to find the best path for your career. His tips on developing personal brand will put you way ahead of your competition. A must read before graduation..."

-Christine Aquin Pope, CEO of GunpowderBusiness and author of *Gunpowder: Ignite your prospecting and accelerate your sales*

"In an open employment market where personal brands and the free agent are changing the meaning of career, it has never been more important to engineer your career plan. Howard Breen's astute personal insights bridge the generational language and offer important, timeless, must-know lessons for people at all stages of their career. ***The Toothpick Factory*** inspires people to really care about marketing themselves and their role as the lead in the most important lifetime performance – their career..."

-Catharine Fennell, CEO, Marketing Yourself Smarter * videoBIO™

"I was lucky to meet Howard Breen in the early stages of my career 20+ years ago. Even then, many people considered Howard the "go-to guy" pertaining to managing one's career. I was one of the benefactors; he has provided me with proven and timeless insights on branding myself, being true to my values, and ultimately leading an organization..."

-Stefan Danis, CEO & Chief Talent Officer Mandrake

"Howard Breen delivers hard-hitting advice to help students steer their way into the working world. His guidelines are sound, insightful and guaranteed to help his readers..."

-David Sculthorpe, President/CEO Canadian Heart and Stroke Foundation

"***The Toothpick Factory*** challenges the young reader to embark on their careers with self-awareness and intention. With experience and authenticity Howard Breen demonstrates the importance of excellence, integrity and responsibility in the building of a successful career and fulfilling life--critical lessons for the young and the 'not-so-young' alike…"

-Susan Marlin, Associate Vice-Principal
(Research), Queen's University

"Hard-hitting, impactful, and seriously good advice. Howard Breen identifies the barriers facing tomorrow's business leaders head on with common sense solutions that make ***The Toothpick Factory*** required reading for those entering or still new to the work force..."

-Barrett Book, President Jump Communications USA

"Imagine if, when you graduated, you had an omniscient spirit guiding you as to exactly what to do for the rest of your career and protecting you from the pratfalls of inexperience and naivety. Written for student and the newly graduated, ***The Toothpick Factory*** is invaluable to anyone embarking upon a new career or avoiding the trap-lines in their current one.

Howard Breen has risen to the top of Canada's advertising industry and provided counsel to many in others. If employees sought and followed Breen's advice, I'd be virtually out of business as an employment lawyer since there are two kinds of employees; those that think before acting and those that get fired…"

-Howard Levitt, Senior Partner, Lang Michener

"Again Howard Breen shares his insights to help the next generation engineer their careers while still in school. The lessons in ***The Toothpick Factory*** hit home and I find myself reading them again and again for my own career…"

-Hugh Samson, Humber School of Business

Praise for "A page from a CEO's Diary"

"Howard Breen offers a compelling, no-nonsense approach to achieving results. ***A page from a CEO's Diary*** is a practical guide with useful exercises to ensure success: an amazing opportunity to learn and grow from his incredible talents. A must-read for leaders across all industries..."

-Robert Leonidas, President/CEO Nestle Canada

"Howard has always been a student of leadership. This book proves that he has learned his lessons well..."

-Richard Peddie, Chairman/CEO Maple Leaf Sports and Entertainment

"***A page from a CEO's Diary*** is an interesting, honest and potentially life-changing account. Howard's words inspire, stimulate self-reflection and offer practical advice for career and life. This book keeps the reader continually engaged..."

-Tony Gagliano, Chairman/CEO St. Joseph Communications

"Powerful and honest: ***A page from a CEO's Diary*** provides straight-forward, invaluable advice. The opportunity to learn from such a dynamic, high-powered executive, as he shares his life experiences with such candor, grace and humor is irresistible..."

-Randy Powell, President/CEO, The Armstrong Group

"Howard's advice on orchestrating careers, moving outside your comfort zone, and finding success will resonate deeply with the reader. He is a highly motivate person who has given the next generation of CEO's a very practical, helpful, but easily readable book..."

-Brent Belzberg, President/CEO, Torquest Partners

"Breen reveals insights based upon his own experiences and achievements. He guides readers through self-assessment and then offers sage, step-by-step advice. **A page from a CEO's Diary** could change your life..."

-Larry Organ, Chairman/CEO ConsumerBase USA

"A very personal collection of thoughts that remind us that being delighted with who we are, and what we have accomplished, is something we choose to do..."

-John Cassaday, CEO Corus Entertainment

"*A page from a CEO's Diary* is provocative, frequently controversial but always entertaining. The lessons are universal. Howard shoots straight from the hip and invites the reader to think about their past, but more importantly to focus on their future..."

-Mike McKelvey, Partner, Borden Ladner Gervais LLP

"A wonderful and insightful compendium of practical knowledge based on Howard's many years of real-life experience as a world-class CEO and a successful business career before that..."

-John Gustuvson, President/CEO Canadian Marketing Association

"Howard is a great story teller and I can hear his voice in these pages. True to form, he has generously shared them now in this very readable and memorable book. His advice on life and work is filled with good ideas, humor, a combination of insight and common sense, and best of all, lots of "Breenisms"..."

-Daryl Aitken, President, Dashboard Communications

"*A page from a CEO's Diary* is the perfect book to read after your last day in school and before your first real job...or for anyone who needs a refresher on finding that elusive balance between life and career..."

-Jacques Duval, Chairman/CEO Marketel Communications

"*A page from a CEO's Diary* is helpful in organizing aspirations, guiding transformation from wishes to reality and ensuring life delivers..."

-Victoria Foley, President, belladonna communications

The Toothpick Factory

Ten Guideposts to help students get the right job

By Howard J. Breen

AuthorHouse™
1663 Liberty Drive
Bloomington, IN 47403
www.authorhouse.com
Phone: 1-800-839-8640

First published by AuthorHouse 5/24/2010

ISBN: 978-1-4520-0338-2 (e)
ISBN: 978-1-4520-0336-8 (sc)
ISBN: 978-1-4520-0337-5 (hc)

Library of Congress Control Number: 2010927276

Printed in the United States of America
Bloomington, Indiana

This book is printed on acid-free paper.

Dedication:

The Toothpick Factory is for my mother, one of those truly selfless people whose abundance of compassion was happily shared with anyone in need.

Forward

My first book, ***A page from a CEO's Diary*** was intended to challenge people to re-evaluate their thinking, values and practices. I've been told that my book made readers laugh, brought them to tears or made them outright frustrated and angry. Several readers were surprised that I shared such personal experiences or had the pugnacity to venture into discussing secrets women should know about men.

Since launching my book, younger readers shared feelings of being overwhelmed with the prospect of entering the job market during such a precarious financial period. University and college students and recent graduates are under immense psychological and emotional pressure from trying to understand how to best enter the "real world" of full-time employment. To some, this is a debilitating time in life. To others, it is creating a profound melancholy and a suffocating despondency.

As such, I decided to write ***The Toothpick Factory*** for younger people who are about to, or who have just entered the work force. Perhaps a few lessons in this book might help to assuage some angst and trepidation by providing clarity on how to approach the job market with a different mindset.

Allow me to explain the title.

I'm a small town boy from a would-be city on the most picturesque of waters, Georgian Bay. It was a fabulous place to embark on life. You knew your neighbors and the great outdoors was just beyond your backyard. Families and community counted for something. For a kid like me, the world around my small town was a magical place full of hope, promise and adventure.

It was necessary to earn money during our summers if we wanted to go to university. My jobs ranged from picking vegetables and fruit, to counting trees for the Ministry of Lands and Forests. I was employed to dye dead coniferous branches to make 'live-looking' artificial Christmas wreaths. I delivered library books to immobile shut-ins and put on puppet plays for children in the city library. I was a week-end proof reader at our local newspaper and installed telephone wire. I also worked as a summer course assistant at The Ivey School of Business at The University of Western Ontario.

Of all my summer jobs, one stands out from the rest. It's where I had the epiphany of my teenage years.

For minimum wage, I worked in a decrepit factory called Keenan Industries. This was one of the few companies in Canada that turned trees into colored swizzle sticks, hospital tongue depressors, Popsicle sticks, shipping pallets and toothpicks.

I dutifully spent an entire summer robotically standing behind an extremely loud chopping machine. I fed veneer (imagine rolls of super thick wooden toilet paper) through a razor-sharp bladed chopper that efficiently cut toothpicks of varying sizes. The noise from the chopping machines was deafening. The monotonous sound of the blades racing up and down was identical to the rat-tat-tat of an AK-47 firing. My job on the toothpick chopper was so mercilessly mundane that the most crucial task was staying awake and keeping all ten fingers attached to my hands. Given what I saw of other workers, not everyone had succeeded at that task.

Being a student, I was not overly welcomed by the full-timers. The seasoned employees considered me one of the spoiled generation. Some of them had been born forty years before me: a number had been born during WWI in 1914-1918. My generation was considered to be hippies and anti-establishment. Our longer hair and propensity to want to be heard made us "delinquents." Our minimum wage was only slightly lower than their hourly wage although they had toiled at the factory for decades.

As one of the "kids," I was relegated to an older toothpick chopper which faced a white-washed brick wall only three feet away. For the record, there were 384 bricks on that wall. There were twenty-five names scratched into the higher level bricks including phone numbers of women who would do really bizarre things for ten bucks.

Accompanying illustrations depicted what you could expect to get for your money.

There was no air-conditioning in the plant and every so often, one of the employees would faint stone-cold from the merciless heat. To allow fresh air into this section of the plant, there was a 12 pane window near my chopper…one of the few benefits of facing the wall. The glass on that 12 pane window was disgustingly filthy. No matter how often a worker would clean it, the glass would return to its grimy state within hours given all the oppressive crap that was floating around the air and infiltrating our lungs. It was loathsome that on our side of that filthy window life was stifling hot when on the outside there was always a cool breeze dancing across the delightfully refreshing bay.

While standing behind that toothpick chopping machine, I spent hour upon endless hour thinking about life. While trying desperately not to succumb to heat prostration, I memorized the order of Prime Ministers, Governor Generals and Presidents of the USA: anything to keep my mind from turning to jelly. I even memorized the Periodic table from front to back and back to front.

I spent a lot of my semi-comatose time analyzing the factory. I witnessed the animosity between the unionized employees and all levels of management. One observation that stuck with me was that older workers would take their time finishing off a job before heading for the exit at the 5:00 pm whistle. The veterans genuinely cared about the output and the quality of their task. They had the best advice in how to get a job done safely and efficiently. The younger employees and in fact, the management of the company, didn't seem to recognize or value their experience or dedication to superior output. The older workers were maliciously labeled, "deadwood."

I observed such waste and inefficiency throughout that factory and wondered how much more money could be earned if the people at the top just stepped back and looked at things differently. It seemed common sense to find more efficient ways of producing toothpicks and tongue depressors, yet no one appeared to want to do anything differently than they had for fifty years. In fact, the company didn't even have an employee suggestion box.

It was at Keenans that I first heard a phrase I would learn to abhor throughout my career. It was that dreadful pat answer to why new ideas were not needed.

"Because that's the way it's always been done around here."

I learned a great deal about business and life in that stifling hot toothpick factory. Now in my 50's, I realize that it was while standing behind those chopping blades, I determined 5 guideposts that held true throughout my entire career: it was like an epiphany for this small town kid. These "5" guideposts became my leitmotifs against which I judged all career decisions and choices.

1. I would arm myself with the right skill set to never again work at such a mundane, mind-killing job.
2. I would be in jobs that allowed me to interface with people of my choice: people I respected and from whom I could learn... regardless of their age or seniority.
3. There was a whole world beyond my toothpick factory and I wanted to experience it. I wanted to be on the correct side of that filthy window.
4. My penchant was going to be identifying more efficient and profitable ways for companies to conduct their businesses. I would never accept the response, "because that's the way it's always been done around here."
5. The best performing teams had a leader who was respected and worked just as hard as every member. I wanted to become one of those leaders.

Now almost forty years after chopping toothpicks, I've had a surprisingly rewarding career rising up the corporate ladder to the CEO's corner office in very large corporations: Quite a journey from facing that whitewashed brick wall trying to avoid having my fingers lopped off.

As you read on, I want you to think about how you are looking at your future and the kind of career you want. I realize that it looks like you are facing an insurmountable wall because of the economic tsunami that has engulfed the world. It's damned scary out there. That's why it's critical that you think about what decisions you will have to make that will affect your success, your health and your relationships.

It is imperative that you take control of your life early in the game.

In the upcoming chapters I'm going to focus on 10 guideposts that helped me throughout my career. These guideposts will be applicable no matter what your course of action: this isn't just about becoming a CEO. It's about finding the right job and then excelling at it from Day One.

I hope you enjoy ***The Toothpick Factory***. If you have questions e-mail me at:

Howard.breen@hbideation.com

Contents

The Toothpick Factory

Chapter 1

Understand your playing field

"Concentrate your strengths against your competitor's relative weaknesses..."

-Bruce Henderson, Boston Consulting Group

As you consider life beyond school, it's vital that you understand what playing field you will be entering. This isn't something you wait until graduation to do. It will be a lot harder to play catch-up then. As a student, you are in an envious position of snatching a much-needed head start on your competition. That is, if you understand the game.

The new playing field you are approaching is laden with opportunities and innumerable minefields. The global economic tsunami that all but collapsed North America's capitalistic backbone is going to be felt far into this next decade. It takes considerable time to recuperate from being kicked in the proverbial financial groin. The recovery we are facing will be long, slow and uphill no matter what the more optimistic financial gurus are professing. However, I've learned that where there are pressures and problems, there are just as many opportunities for those armed with the right attitude and skill sets.

This first chapter is going to help you understand your new playing field so you can recalibrate your thinking on how best to arm yourself. This chapter will examine the roles that globalization and demographics will play as you engineer your career.

1. Globalization and the digital generation

The working world you will be, or have just entered, is dramatically different than the one on which my generation cut its teeth. You are now truly entering a global stage with opportunities and a geographically limitless workforce. Your playing field is not Toronto, Chicago, Montreal or New York. It's so much greater and more exciting if you can understand that globalization is going to offer opportunities and risks to your generation like never before in history. It isn't a dream anymore. It's a hard core reality.

Throughout history, the concept of globalization has had different faces. In the 15th Century, Zhu Di, Emperor of China commissioned almost 2000 ships to sail the oceans and bring the world into China's fold. His fleet included the famous 'treasure ships,' and interestingly carried as many artisans, philosophers, and traders as they did soldiers and sailors. The Emperor envisioned China extending its reach around the planet to gather greater wealth in monetary, cultural and knowledge terms. But there was something even deeper and more fascinating in his reasoning. Zhu Di felt that in order to build Chinese financial domination globally, it was mandatory to share "China." Zhu Di understood that extending his financial empire could only be achieved by setting up a network that interchanged communication, philosophy, art and most importantly, culture. The ships set sail and there is much evidence that a number of his fleet reached North and South America in the early 1400's, far earlier that their European counterparts.

Alas, Zhu Di's heartfelt vision of globalization failed miserably. The Emperor was politically outmaneuvered by powerful financial controllers who felt a global vision and reach would threaten the very core of the Empire. They reasoned that China's future and cultural superiority was better protected by adhering to Confucian principles that included a more inward and conservative focus: inside the wall. They feared the return of the fleet and the cancerous impact that foreign learning and new knowledge might have on everything they held sacred in China. The financial mandarins fought Zhu Di at every step of the way. They ambushed the Emperor by creating financial and political obstacles that were insurmountable. The country faced bankruptcy and the threat of war from neighboring nations that Zhu Di had made a practice of excluding or abusing in the past. Before his dream could be realized Zhu Di died, the ships were recalled and China stepped back behind the wall.

Imagine for a moment what would have happened if Zhu Di had better controlled his enemies and had succeeded in his vision of a transportation, communication and cultural network around the world? What language would we all be speaking today? What religious beliefs would we be teaching our children? Zhu Di's vision of globalization was formulated almost 600 years ago!

In the mid-17th Century, under Elizabeth I, England ruled the global trade game through their far-travelling ships, conscription, superior knowledge of seafaring and of course, advanced weaponry. The ships of Her Majesty's Royal Navy could facilitate trade wherever their fleets could sail. They quickly deployed their military might, customs and language. British imperialistic rule clawed out into every corner of the planet and it was true that the sun never set on the British Empire. Unlike Zhu Di whose vision was to share learning and culture, the British rulers felt that a "one-way" conversation would be more prosperous and beneficial to England. For the next 300 years English Sovereigns reinforced with might that the English language, culture, customs, laws, dress and philosophies were indisputably better than anything else on the planet. Their canons, rifles, and Governors made it difficult for conquered nations to disagree. This was another face of globalization: one way and driven through transportation and military might.

In the 1800s, the world shifted as the United States entered the global game after defying and defeating English rule. Shipping and transportation opened up new trade routes and alliances: both political and economic. Immigration sent Europeans and Asians to North America in the millions and soon customs and histories began to blend. Markets opened in the East for Western products and in the West for Eastern products. Shipping and military might continued to drive globalization but soon the advent of the telegraph and steam altered the role and speed of communication and transportation.

In the early to mid 1900's the world lived at geographically expansive war, divvying up geography and changing the face of the political landscape. Nuclear weaponry created a stalemate of a Cold War for close to forty years after the end of WWII. In that century, the speed and modes of transportation changed through horse-less carriages, to steam-travel, to airplanes, to jets, to nuclear power and then men walking on the moon. High speed trains soon connected England to Europe through the Chunnel. Shipping had been relegated to transportation of goods although nuclear submarines and city-sized aircraft carriers continue to promote gunboat diplomacy.

But of all inventions in the 1900s, it has been the development of communication vehicles that has altered the face of the planet and how politics and business are conducted. From early telephones, to televisions, to faxes, communication assumed a new role. Reaching new markets and consumers became achievable at the push of a button. Corporations jumped on the opportunity to extend their reach and drive sales into new untapped foreign markets. How easy was it for American and European companies to send their own skilled labor abroad to run offices in Bombay, Beijing or Sri Lanka? How financially astute was it to use less expensive off-shore talent to produce goods and products that could then be sold in the States or Europe at a hefty premium? The business world of ex-patriots flourished and a business blueprint unfolded for globalization. The speed of communication became king. Once again, the pen was mightier than the sword.

By the 1980s the global playing field exploded with a new 'device' that would change the face of the planet. It would unhinge everything we had learned up to that point about conducting business globally. The explosive growth of the internet and personal computer restructured our way of life in mere decades. This was akin to the outcomes of Britain's industrial revolution being conducted on a keyboard by a ten year-old kid after school. Imagine taking the room-sized computers NASA employed for the moon landing in 1969 and replacing them through chip technology with a laptop and a Blackberry. This is the playing field you are about to enter.

With the arrival of the internet, the world opened up to powerful international business alliances...mainly driven from within the borders of the United States. In the mid to late 20th Century, globalization (for all intensive purposes) meant Americanization of business procedures, accounting practices, marketing and currency. It also meant American ex-patriots conducting operations throughout the world...according to American business practices.

During the same time frame in the 20th Century, the political landscape underwent dramatic earthquakes with the demise of the "Cold War," the well-choreographed collapse of the Soviet Union, the inevitable fall of the Berlin Wall, the horrifying 'coming of age' of the terrorist threat, and the much vaunted 're-awakening' of China as a global financial powerhouse player.

Enough of the history lessons: What does this have to do with you? Simply that your job prospects don't just include North America and it is vital that you adjust your filters to become more globally aware if you hope to comprehend your playing field. This new 'arena' represents opportunities as well as competition from students graduating from universities all over the world.

As updated by the U.S. Census Bureau in June, 2008, here is how the world's population sits. I've specifically presented the USA and Canada in juxtaposition with the developing countries as considered as Brazil, Russia, India and China (BRIC):

Ranking	Country	Population (billions)
1.	China	1.33
2.	India	1.15
3.	USA	.304
4	Brazil	.196
5.	Russia	.140
6.	Canada	.033

Even with the passage of the first decade of the 21st Century, the global paradigm has shifted again. 9/11 showed a vulnerability of the most prolific money-making machine on the planet. Almost coincident with the horrors of 9/11 came another onslaught to the capitalistic foundation of America. It seemed that every week in 2008 and 2009 a CEO was arrested and charged for breaching accounting ethics and practices. Shareholder value in companies was massacred and the public confidence in our governments and financial mandarins dissolved. Doors began closing at venerable financial institutions and we learned about sub-prime mortgages and toxic assets. Analysts jumped up saying 'I told you so' while the world stock exchanges collapsed and everyone ran for cover. CEOs looked like deer caught in the headlights and governments stepped in with bail out dollars that our children will be paying off long after we're all six feet under.

In his book, "House of Cards," author William D. Cohan takes us inside the collapse of a number of venerable financial institutions, particularly Bear Stearns as he offers, "the financial industry had become so paralyzed by self-inflicted wounds by March, 2008." We had a real awakening as to what happens when greed, envy, and utter stupidity battle each other in the minds of the power brokers.

These threats to our personal well-being and financial security rocked our confidence in the ability of our leaders and governments to protect our way of living and our future security. For those born after the great depression, we had a wake-up call like never before: even including the Great Depression of the 1930's.

These events of the first decade of the 21st Century have incited a complete recalibrating what "globalization" means today.

The world at large has shifted monumentally as non-North American based 'international' companies have upped their game with improved financing; stronger infrastructures; a longer-termed focus on product superiority; lower cost structures; more flexible employee standards; and, a more realistic perspective on globalization. BRIC (Brazil, Russia, India and China) companies are catching up and surpassing their North American and European counterparts. Emerging nation's companies no longer are just out-sourcing destinations. They are strong and vibrant producers of outstanding quality.

Globalization no longer means Americanization, and the word "international" takes on a totally different perspective depending on the longitude and latitude of your country. International companies are redefining the planet and you need to carefully understand who these players are on this global playing field.

Anybody bought a Toyota lately? How about any product from Sony, Yue Yuen or Tata? There are now more companies from outside the USA moving into the Fortune 500 than any time in history. In 20 years I predict that more than 30% of the Fortune 500 will be international (as in non North American based).

Anyone who doesn't understand this global shift need only Google companies in Russia like Gazprom: the largest Russian company (actually it is owned by the government) which at the time of printing this book had over 445,000 employees; a market capitalization of $348 Billion (as reported in June, 2009 US F/X); and is the world's biggest owner of natural gas. It has businesses including banking, insurance, construction, agriculture and media.

And while there are American interests in Russian oil, it was China who in the summer of 2009 announced a $25 Billion investment in Russia's biggest oil producer and its pipeline operator in exchange for business considerations. What a wonderful way for China to use its financial power to secure natural resources for its exploding economy. While China's economy has been weathering the global financial storm, its ability to grow domestically will serve it much better than export-rich economies. If you want to see the most incredible example of a real life Monopoly board game at play, follow the investments of Chinese interests. In the October, 2009 issue of Fortune, Bill Powell wrote, "So far this decade China has spent an estimated $115 billion of foreign acquisitions. Now that the nation is sitting on massive foreign-exchange wealth ($2.1 trillion and counting), it is eager to find something (anything!) to invest in besides U.S. Treasury debt. In 2008, China's investments abroad doubled from $25 billion to $50 billion."

But beyond China's financial investment posture, what else must they do to ascend onto the global stage in this century? For this answer, the current Chinese leaders must remember Zhu Di's vision 600 hundred years ago. He envisioned China's ascension on the global stage being achieved by balancing wealth creation with cultural, philosophical and artist expression: extending Chinese finances and culture externally while reaping foreign finances and culture at the same time. **Enduring financial growth will not be achieved by China simply by financially investing in countries outside the wall.** There are some business analysts that criticize China for become the "world's factory." I think that's hardly the case anymore given their buying spree into natural resources, banking, health-care, electronics, transportation, real-estate, utilities and manufacturing in every continent on the planet.

As a sub-text, China's biggest leaps forward will come when they dedicate the same investment inside the wall in their cultural, philosophical and artistic underpinnings. It will mean: telling their legions of censors to stand down; investing in artist endeavors like 798 in Beijing; and, proving to the world that they allow free thinking and speech.

In a different part of the world, Brazil is leading the way of South American companies extending their reach from beyond the southern hemisphere. Google a Brazilian corporation named 'Vale' and read about a mining company with over 100,000 employees that is sewing up the mining industry globally.

In India, Tata is a business conglomerate with 96 companies and over 350,000 employees. It includes companies in these industries: agricultural chemicals and tools; automotive components; watches; beverages; air travel; telecommunication; insurance and financial services; retail; television; hotels; food additives and jewelry.

If you have recently purchased Nike, Adidas, Reebok, Asics, New Balance or Pumas, the odds are that part, or all of those shoes you bought passed through a company in China called Yue Yuen. This is one of China's largest companies with two major shareholders: the Tsai Family and Pou Chen Corporation. Aside from being an OEM for sports and casual shoes, it has retail operations and also manufactures components for amps.

As this longer-term global realignment is unfolding you can view this as a deterioration of what we know and how things have been or, you can look at this as a wake-up call and:

1. **Determine what opportunities and risks await you as you enter the global playing field.** Keep in mind that there is an influx of digital generation talent from all over the world…not just North America;

2. Watch how our Canadian governments begin to dance with each member of BRIC. On the day I'm writing this, our Prime Minister is in China trying to get Canada on a preferred supplier and tourist destination list. The Premier of Ontario is in India trying to secure new business contracts for firms focusing on efficient energy and production. Understand the implications for the industry you are considering joining;

3. Be en garde as North American companies shift their hiring practices towards non North American graduates who are

coming with a lower salary expectation that their North Am counterparts;

4. Set up international information and learning networks between your university and the top schools in each of BRIC;

5. Start following what is happening outside of North America and construct files on the biggest players on the world business stage;

6. Evaluate your skill set and make some hard decisions how you can better arm yourself to be more competitive and productive than your counterparts graduating outside of our continent; and,

7. Realize that the first job you get may not even exist today. New industries requiring new talent are popping up as I write these words. I envy you this new frontier and hope that the upcoming chapters might help clarify your thinking and approach as you embark on your job and career journey.

2. Demographics and the Digital Generation

As you proceed through university and college (or have just entered the work force) you will need to understand the playing field from a generational perspective. You will be entering a work force with people with different skill sets and diverse attitudes than your own. Not everyone is going to welcome you with open arms and a generous spirit.

Let me give you an example by looking at my own "baby boomer" generation. I guarantee you are going to find this rather amusing (and in some ways frightening) because it is people like me who are going to be running the companies at which you might find yourself looking for a job.

As a baby boomer growing up in Canada, I was indoctrinated to know these "supposedly" irrefutable truths:

> you need to diligently and patiently work your way up the ladder to succeed. If the company needs you to work overtime then you should do it without complaint;

> it's okay to have lots of kids because jobs are plentiful and governments have excellent health care and pension plans;

> the parents are the heads of the families and children need to listen to what they say and teach;

> English language and customs over anything;

> religious leaders as unquestioned pillars of the community;

> the best products and thinking come from American companies and crappier products come from China or Japan;

> relationships are about 'men and women'...anything else is wrong;

> there is a glass ceiling that prevents women from moving 'too far' up the corporate ladder;

> good always triumphs over evil and the bad guy always get nailed;

> our political leaders know what they are doing;

> big companies will look out for the welfare of their employees; and,

> as General Motors goes, so does the American government.

Our athletes were the best because our MLB World Series, Stanley Cup and Super Bowl were 'global' championships. Budweiser was the King of Beers; Elvis was the King of Rock & Roll; Clark Gable was the King of Hollywood; and, Michael Jackson was the King of Pop. All the big awards were North American like the Academy Awards, The Emmys, The Grammys, and The Tonys.

Frightening isn't it because you are about to enter a workforce with a whole bunch of senior employees and business leaders who were cut from the same cloth as me. **You are going to have to understand that as a member of the Digital Generation, you are going to be the anomaly.** I'm amazed at the number of younger employees who are entering the workforce and walking blindly into generational issues:

they aren't grasping the importance of understanding that their co-workers don't really understand them.

You need to be aware of the minefields created by the generational playing field. Jim Morrison, the leather-clad, crotch-grabbing lead singer of The Doors said that, "Each generation wants new symbols, new people, new names. They want to divorce themselves from their predecessors." I certainly did and now I watch my daughter's generation trying their best to divorce themselves from mine. That's just the way it goes.

A recurring question by many business leaders pertains to dealing with the arrival of your cyber-programmed generation…the Digital Generation: aka Gen Y, Echo Boomers, Net Geners, Internet Generation or Digital Kids. Business leaders are anxiously trying to figure out how to get the best out of you knowing that the global workforce is deteriorating as boomers exit in the hundreds of millions. On the other side of coin, you need to be considering how to find your way through a gauntlet of other generations who aren't readily prepared or technologically-armed to embrace you.

While you may not want to hear this, your generation is coming to the light with a very questionable reputation. Everyone seems to concur that you are the first generation bred 'through' a computer. Your technical expertise is unquestioned. Your ability to rise up en masse to counter a faulty product, a political misstep or a social injustice is remarkable. When I watch my son or daughter rocket their way through websites, YouTube and Facebook, I marvel at their grasp of how to gather information in nano-seconds that would have taken months when I was their age. How your generation is making use of social media is mind-boggling. It's great how you are connecting but do you realize how much of yourself you are giving away with photos and stories that might come back to haunt you in years to come? I spoke at a university a month ago and asked the audience of 600+ a question: How many of you would forward your current Facebook account to a potential employer and not have any concerns about what they might see or read? Only 20 students put up their hands saying they had no concerns. The rest lowered their heads or looked sheepishly at each other. Some giggled and found my question humorous.

There are many, many positives that other generations see in you but there are just as many negatives. In talking with a plethora of CEOs and senior business executives, the concerns are shared. Almost to a person, they view your generation as a problem: coddled, spoiled, entitled, naïve, socially-challenged with unrealistic expectations concerning pay and the time needed to be invested for a promotion. You are considered ill-mannered, childish and willing to live off your parents as long as they'll put up with you. Known to jump from one job to another, you aren't considered loyal or dedicated. While most leaders have no hard-core statistics to support their viewpoint, they feel you abuse the company by 'surfing the web' for excessive amounts of time.

Doesn't sound fair, does it? Realize this is the demographic playing field upon which you are entering.

Don Tapscott's latest book 'grown up digital' is all about you and I'd encourage you to pick up a copy. Mr. Tapscott surveyed over 11,000 people and his results were very surprising if not controversial: "instead of a bunch of spoiled 'screenagers' with short attention spans and zero social skills, he discovered a remarkably bright community which has developed revolutionary new ways of thinking, interacting, working, and socializing."

But this is not the experience of many generations witnessing your inflow into the workforce. Let me illustrate this with a short story.

A CEO named Kathleen Porter is an entrepreneur who owns a company that manufactures components for televisions, video games and cellular phones. VistaComs employs 485 employees and has been in business for thirty years. Business took a real revenue and bottom-line hit with the economic tsunami of 2008-09. There have been staff layoffs and Kathleen is looking to save money. Beyond the budgeted staff cuts, the company has had considerable employee turnover with employees aged 30 and under. The exit interviews clearly show that Porter's company is out of touch with the 'Net Gener' employees on her payroll. To help formulate her thinking around some pending changes to the benefits' package, the CEO calls a meeting with a representative of each of the five generations that make up her staff:

1. 68 year old Len Miller has been with VistaComs for 29 years. He will not be retiring at 65 because he needs the company medical plan for his wife Grace, who is battling cancer. Len was born in 1941 during WWII. His family got their first television

set when he was fourteen: it was a black and white screen and had one television station that shut down at midnight. Len is not a fan of computers but has a cell phone. He never learned to type.

2. At 53, Monica Greenwood is the top end of the Baby Boomer generation and has been with the company for 17 years. Monica's husband Irwin retired 4 years ago and they have three kids: two of whom are in college. Monica was born in 1956, the year that Elvis Presley had his first #1 hit on the Billboard charts. Monica uses her Blackberry but still needs her assistant to prepare her power point presentations.

3. Frank Thomas is the bottom end (Echo) of the Baby Boomers at 46 and has been with VistaComs for 10 years. Frank is married and has a son in university and a daughter in High School. Frank was born five days after John Kennedy was assassinated in Dallas, Texas. Frank is fluent digitally and has been instrumental in pushing VistaComs into the 21st Century business mode.

4. Having just turned 38, Jonathon Chen is in the Gen X group. He and his life partner Jacob adopted twins last year. Jonathon has been with the company for 8 years and is on the fast track for a senior management position. Jonathon was born the year Jimmy Hendrix died. Jon is a typical Gen Xer feeling disconnected with the baby boomers.

5. 26 year old Susan Franklin is the 'Digital Generation' representative. Susan joined VistaComs a year ago. She's already had two previous jobs since graduating from university four years ago. Susan is single and has had some strains acclimatizing to the company. She has been shocked by the iniquities of the office and the oppressive nature of the people in charge. *(Susan is about five or six years older than you are. She shares a lot of your attitudes and obvious technical skills).*

As their CEO calls the meeting to order, the six attendees settle down. Frank turns off his Blackberry as Susan finishes replying to a text message from a friend in New York with whom she is planning a trip. Kathleen explains the meeting is to discuss having the employees pay for part of their benefits cost. The recent financial downturn means expenses have to be reduced. One outlay that can be 'addressed' is to have the employees contribute 25% of the cost of their health benefits. Kathleen says she is seeking input on how best to 'sell' this to her employees. She asks for candor and sits back.

The first to pipe up is Susan Franklin. The Gen Y'er has no issues speaking her mind in front of the CEO or anyone else. She is abound with confidence and doesn't like to waste time. Susan has no burning loyalty to this company and the fact they are about to screw her out of money is exactly what she has been raised to believe corporate America is all about.

"I'm not surprised by any of this," Susan begins. "This company doesn't seem to want to keep its best workers. I frankly won't be able to afford to stay here if I'm now going to be nailed to pay for benefits that I don't even use. Why don't you just cut the overall benefits and give the employees the money to get the benefits they need? I could use that money in twenty different ways rather than pay for benefits I don't need."

Len sits forward imperiously. He is a very conservative man and his loyalty to the firm is well-known. Susan reminds him of his mentally imbalanced grandchildren: all talk without a lot of deep substance. Always glued to their computers and music and so spoiled it made him sick. Manners like barbarians and toxic with their attitudes.

"Young lady, there are a lot of people who started working here before you were born. I'm one of them. These older employees rely heavily on the benefit package for medical and dental. If the company needs us to contribute given the global economic meltdown then that's what we do."

"I don't agree with that Len," Jonathon Chen interjects firmly, but with genuine diffidence to the older employee. "Len, this isn't just about age or tenure. I can't afford to kick in 25% and I don't want to give up any medical or dental benefits. I've got two new babies at home. What if we made more staff cuts to protect the welfare of our current staff?

The CEO shakes her head. "No Jon, it's got to be this way."

The room is quiet until the Gen Y'er speaks up again. Trying to collaborate has been ingrained in her nature. She isn't intimidated by seniority. The others don't understand this and feel she is being disrespectful.

"Look, there has to be a way to cut out un-necessary benefits. Why don't you have a list of benefits that employees can pick from and then pay exactly that cost? Why should I have to pay for benefits having to do with families and kids when I'm not even married?" Susan sits back and folds her arm. Her Blackberry vibrates and she picks it up. The others in the room watch as she reads an email.

"Susan, hold off on your messages until the meeting is over," Kathleen directs politely, and Susan begrudgingly agrees. Turning off her connectivity with the world is like being asked to stand in the corner.

The company's Head of HR, notices that the girl's phone is still turned on. Karen Jolly has had a number of encounters with Susan Franklin and is concerned that there are many younger employees with her same distorted view of their self-worth and sense of entitlement. Just last week, Susan showed up in the HR department and impertinently demanded a 45% raise and an extra week's holiday so she could travel with friends. The HR leader realized that everything she had been reading about this new generation was bang on. The sense of entitlement was bred into them from the first time they got a ribbon for finishing in 8th place in Grade 2. These new kids had been funded by parents who paid the whole ticket for university and bought their 'children' anything their hearts desired. What absurdity. And now, with such a spoiled attitude, they wouldn't put in overtime and the thought of displaying any loyalty or seeking longevity was completely foreign to them. Hell, she knew that Susan was still living at home with her folks. What a leach! Most of these new kids were like a malignant disease feeding off the organization and dampening moral.

Karen Jolly is 57 and one of Kathleen's first hires. She stared scrupulously at Susan and then looked out the window and remembered easier times. Clouds were moving in from the south-west and Karen wondered if she had closed the windows on the second floor of her house.

Frank Thomas clears his throat and gingerly enters the discussion.

Susan has no time for Frank since she overheard him comment

that the new kids did nothing all day except play on their computers checking out web-sites and connecting with their friends. Susan considers him one of the biggest jerks in the company.

"Our medical bills are already paralyzing our family. I can't put 25% into the benefits and I can't have any of them taken away. Kathleen, this would damage our family and I've been here for ten years. There has to be another way."

At this point, Susan has withdrawn from the meeting. She is reflectively thinking about a competitive company with whom she interviewed three weeks ago. They offered her an extra $7,000 per annum and an extra week's holidays. She wasn't even sure what their benefit package was but the company was geographically closer to her apartment which would cut out travel time. They also had more flexible working hours and gave everyone a Blackberry and unlimited texting.

Monica Greenwood sat forward and raised her hand.

"There is an element of fair play here. Look at this room. We are all at different stages in our careers and our family lives. People like Frank and Jon need more benefits. Susan is single without kids and is being asked to pay 25% towards something she doesn't need, or want. Isn't that right Susan?"

Susan nods and casually looks down at the screen on her phone considering the other people in the room. What a monstrously inept group of old farts, she muses.

"But there will be a lot of employees who can't kick in 25%," Monica continued. "This economic recession hasn't just hit VistaComs. It's hit every one of us with extra costs like gas and food prices. Kathleen, a benefit plan that treats everyone as if they have the same needs just doesn't make sense. We need to recognize that in our company are five distinctive generations with different medical needs. If you force a 25% contribution, I'd be surprised if you keep one person of Susan's genre here in the next 3 months."

Karen Jolly looked at Susan and asked, "Is that correct Susan?"

"Absolutely," Susan confirmed defiantly, crossing her arms in exasperation. "I don't want to seem disloyal but I would be out of here as soon as I could find a new job. You guys have to catch up with what's happening in the world. Instead of focusing on health care costs, you should be looking up updating your computers and all the red tape around here. It's all about speed and this company is so slow it's ridiculous. My home computer is better than anything we have in this building."

"Kathleen," Frank respectfully interjected, disregarding what he viewed to be impertinence and unprofessionalism in the girl. "There has to be another way. What if we just reduced the benefit programs for the younger employees like Susan who don't use them anyway?"

"What?" Susan laughed facetiously, as she picked up her phone and quickly looked at the most recent text message. "That's really typical. Just because I'm single and don't have a family you don't think I have expenses. I still have some student loans to take care of. Why should I have to give up anything for you? I'm already underpaid in this company."

"Well, perhaps because you really haven't had enough time in this company to have earned your rightful place anyway," sniped Len Mill with contempt, thinking back on his 29 years of service and wondering why this deluded pup was even allowed to attend a meeting of such importance. "Hell, we all know you still live at home so it's not like you're paying rent or anything. I can't count the number of times I've walked past your cubicle listened to you laughing and carrying on while you are at your computer. Lord knows what you are doing all day."

And with that, the room erupted into several meetings. It was abundantly clear that there would be no easy resolution. Kathleen sat forward and raised her hand to bring the meeting back to order. Feeling paralyzed she wondered, "Perhaps it is time to sell the company. I've got enough money put away. Do I really need to put up with all this foolishness?"

*

I've exaggerated Susan's role of the Net Gener but I've personally witnessed behavior very close to hers and the other people in the room. When you read this scenario, it was Susan who actually came up with the most logical approach to solving the core issue. Unfortunately, her method of delivery and the room's prejudice towards her generation clouded her ability to be truly heard or accepted.

This 'blending of generations' is a common issue facing companies. While I've simplified the gravity of this potential crisis with Kathleen,

Karen, Susan, Len, Frank, Monica and Jonathon, you can imagine how deeply the differences are felt on a daily basis. Companies are being damaged with un-needed staff turnover and are not recognizing that their employee base must be dealt with differently. **The workplace has become a treacherous landscape where Net Geners' instinctive spontaneity and candor can incinerate a career.**

In 2003, a very intriguing book was published entitled, "When Generations Collide: Who They Are, Why They Clash, How to Solve the Generational Puzzle at Work." It was co-penned by Lynne Lancaster and David Stillman. Considering we are now seven years after they released their research findings, consider how much more intensified this problem has become. Lancaster and Stillman wrote, "We listened to Boomers complain how they had given years to a company only to be passed over or laid off in favor of younger employees who were more knowledgeable about technology and cost less money. We heard Gen Xers protest how they were being treated like slackers and ask why other generations didn't like them. We spoke with Millennials who told us they couldn't stand being put in the same category as Gen Xers and wanted to be judged on their own merits."

When I started out I was a lot like your generation. I wanted a challenge and a chance to contribute. I tried not to be belligerent when I was faced with institutionalized procedures that were archaic and designed to slow down the most controlled of hyper-achievers. I was very impatient for promotions and raises and I'm sure I drove my supervisors to distraction questioning them why I was being held back. It drove me to distraction when I was told, "that's the way it is around here." Well, sometimes that phrase was my inspiration to find a new job because to me it wasn't a moral dilemma. It was just bad business that I wouldn't allow to hold me back.

Conventional wisdom is that your generation is impatient with timelines, falseness and any form of corporate B.S. I think that's a good thing if it's kept in perspective and doesn't dwell on being relentlessly irritable. Don't be willing to accept timelines just because "that's the way it is around here." But then, don't be so foolish or naïve to be demanding foolish or unreasonable perks, titles or raises if you haven't earned them.

I can't foresee any company dealing only with one generation of employees. I don't care if their focus and products are high tech or broom manufacturers. **In order to get the best out of their employees, business leaders need to hire staff that reflects society and the age/sex/ethnicity of the clients and customers.** For many senior managers, this will require a complete rethink of hiring practices, training and education procedures, company policies on holiday recognition, policies on sexual harassment, their policies on age discrimination, and their policies of fair play across all ethnic and religious groups. It will also require a relook of remuneration and benefits.

So what does this all mean to you as you have, or are about to enter the workforce?

1. Recognize that the company you've joined is going to have to change the way in which they've conducted business in the past. Employees and customers are completely different animals than they were 5-10 years ago. Employees must be treated more individually and not as a collective with the same goals, desires, capabilities and needs. Customers must not be preached to.

2. **Know that there will be senior people who will have preconceived notions about you as being spoiled and petulant with an undeserved sense of entitlement.** You know more about computers and internet and that represents a risk to the status quo. Some people just don't like change.

3. Before you sign on with a company, investigate how they are blending the various skills and experiences of cross generations. Don't be shy in asking how the company sets up teams of varying ages or how they encourage new thinking to be brought forward by your generation. Ask about benefits packages and how they are customized to employees' circumstances and needs.

4. Understand that gender equality is not a nice thing to do in business: it's mandatory. As the boomer bubble moves into retirement, countries and companies will have no choice but to use the best and brightest they can hire which shouldn't have a lot to do with whether the employee is male or female. In a world where technical superiority and collaboration trumps

brute strength, females must be given equal footing, pay and opportunities.

5. When you enter a company, be respectful of everyone you meet regardless of how they react to your arrival. Get to know the strengths that are the foundation of your new place of employment. It's easy to find faults but a lot harder to step back and give credit for all the good things that are taking place. If you see areas that are broken or could be working better then it's your job to bring ideas forward. Consider carefully how to raise those issues and your ideas. Perhaps you could enlist the help of more seasoned employees for their counsel on how best to convey your thinking.

6. Be prepared to have a work computer that isn't as good as your own at home. Companies try to get the most of every computer before they have to expend capital dollars to upgrade.

7. Don't discount the way you look at the world, social relationships and the internet. **Your generation has a wealth of experience that companies need to bring on board in order to survive. Don't sell yourself short.** Recognize that about 50% of your senior people will not be familiar with Twitter, Facebook or any form of social media. 30% have probably have never sent a text message or bought anything on-line. Don't mock it. Offer suggestions on how to initiate training programs.

8. Make yourself an expert on understanding the machinations of each generation of employees working in the company. Importantly, understand how each generation does/does not interact with each other. Perhaps you can become a facilitator to assist the company. Collaboration is in your blood.

9. **Don't allow your attitude to interfere with bringing forward great ideas and new thinking**. You will face roadblocks. That's part of the game of being the youngest on the totem pole. Similarly, don't be intimidated by age or seniority. Be respectful, but not afraid. A.P. Gouthey wrote, "If life were measured by accomplishments, most of us would die in infancy."

10. Similarly, be very clear in understanding your company's expectations of all employees, including its newest arrivals. Make sure they use very unambiguous language about the job's accountabilities, reporting, training, expectations for salary increases, promotions, and overtime. Read the binder of company policies you are given. **Ignorance is no excuse for error.** How transparent are the leaders? Is there a way you can have your job description customized for you? What special or peculiar skills do you have that could be incorporated into it?

Chapter 1 Highlight:

The new global reality is a borderless playing field which requires you to remove geographic blinders. The opportunities are phenomenal for those with vision. With opportunity comes risk as a plethora of highly talented students graduating outside North America see you as competition. Many North American companies are looking at those students who cost less than you.

Be aware of the multi-generational mine-field you are about to enter. A lot of senior people grew up thinking having a television clicker was hot technology. You have so much to bring to the table if you keep it in the proper perspective and use your collaborative skills.

Chapter 2

Personally brand yourself

"He who has conquered himself by the Self, he is a friend of himself; but he whose Self is unconquered, his self acts as his own enemy like an external foe..."

-Bhagavad Gita (4th-3rd century B.C.)

Once you understand your playing field you need to step back and take a look in the mirror. A lot of people don't like what they see in that mirror but they don't do anything about it. Given the complexities of the new playing field it is vital that you do whatever it takes to like and admire the person you see; and, to believe that this person is the best person you can possibly be. Anything less is going to leave you feeling unfulfilled in your career and your personal relationships.

In this chapter I want to talk about looking in that mirror and understanding the role that branding plays in helping yourself be the best person you can be.

I've spent a 30+ year career in Canada and the United States helping companies brand their products. There are few product categories that I have not played a role in branding and marketing. I've worked with incredible organizations in helping to match, or create a consumer need for a product. Untold billions of dollars have been spent promoting branding to get Consumer X to buy Product Y...and then to buy it again. I've watched companies reap the financial benefits of intelligently branding their products. I've watch companies fail miserably by either promoting a weak product or poorly promoting a good product in an un-motivating manner.

In the past ten years, the way in which marketers are interacting with consumers has changed monumentally with the advent of the internet, customized television stations and the explosive growth of hand-held mobile devices. Manufacturers have had to dramatically re-invent their marketing machines for a much more consumer-savvy target base: purchasers not willing to accept mediocrity or excessive pricing given their ability to go on-line and investigate everything about anything. **Manufacturers now have to pay attention to consumers because it's no longer a one way conversation at the consumer...it's now consumers talking to each other about the product and the company itself.** It's about customers going on-line and telling the world about your product, your business ethics and morals and whether you and your product are worth buying. And that is how today's companies are being made and broken.

But this chapter is not about creating consumer demand or branding products. This chapter is about branding people: specifically about branding you.

Successful people brands are a business and those businesses must be developed, nurtured and protected. **The top people brands on this planet are licenses to print money.** Look at the Beatles, Bono, Taylor Swift, Beyonce, Lady Gaga, Paris Hilton, Nicole Kidman, Bill Gates, Mariah Carey, Warren Buffet, Jennifer Lopez, Michael Jordan, and every major business figure or athlete. These celebrities get paid to simply show up. The endorsements ring up on their cash registers for the power of their name and positioning. They speak and people listen. They wear a clothing item or perfume and people run out to buy it. These breathing and living brands do very little by chance and are overly careful to guard their image.

In the book, 'The Age of Persuasion: How Marketing Ate our Culture' authors Terry O'Reilly and Mike Tennant write, "Stars are protective of their brands. They know what enhances it and what does not. That's why stars refuse to do anything that's not in their brand's character." I think someone should have reminded Tiger Woods of this little tidbit of advice.

In the world of people brands I believe that one of the most innovative branders on the planet for the last three decades has been Madonna. For more than 20 years I have studied her orchestrate, and maneuver her brand. If you want to see beautiful personal branding at its best, log onto Madonna.com.

Madonna and her business gurus have nailed it. How else do you keep on the top of the charts with such a fickle, age-changing target over three decades? How do break the 50 year age bracket and still be considered one of the hottest females strutting this planet?

I think Madge's "5 guideposts" might look like this:

1. Relentlessly drive the focus on great music while appearing to be ahead of the trends.

2. Never forget your core ability (which in Madonna's case is to dance her competition into the ground).

3. Reach new younger audiences to fill the "pipeline" (the impetus behind the dozen children's books that Madonna has penned?)

4. Do not be constrained by geographic borders, language issues or technology (check out the website for her videos, posters, DVD's, CDs and over twenty movies in which Madonna has starred in, or directed).

5. Carefully orchestrate and extend the music/dance brand into other relevant product lines: clothing, furniture and 'logoed' products.

With these 5 guideposts, it's easy to see why Madonna continues to outperform her competition and ring the cash register. Doubtless, that a well-crafted people brand reaps serious financial benefits in life.

Have you considered your own personal brand? What is it that all these manufacturers and world-class personalities know that you don't? Why do they focus so much attention on their product offering, their packaging, their positioning, and their audiences? **It's time for you to seriously consider the value of your own brand.** I fear that the vast majority of people are not taking the time needed to focus on their personal brand. They complain about one obstacle after another: school work, family, friends or the new job vampire all their time.

For a lot of these people, it may be too late to try to revamp and re-launch their own personal branding efforts. While not impossible, it gets harder to make significant changes in your life when you have family and financial commitments. It's also very difficult to change how people look at you when they have already formed their opinion of you (and your brand) over a lengthy period of time. That's why I'm writing this book for students and young people just out of school.

Do you realize that people around you form opinions about you and your personal brand? That's why it's so vital when you are starting out in your business life that you determine what your brand is...before others determine it for you. Who are these others? They are your target audiences.

We all have target audiences: families, significant others, schoolmates, professors, new bosses, co-workers, neighbors and friends. **Your target audiences will form opinions of you based on how you behave and how you interact with them.**

Here is a question for you.

Do your various target audiences look at you the way you see yourself? Do they believe you are the person you think you are inside? I want you to consider this very seriously and by the time we are through, you need to "know" the answer to this question. I don't want you to "believe you know" the answer. I want you only dealing in facts.

Do people see you the way you see yourself?

You might find this interesting, but most people automatically answer affirmative. They believe they represent themselves optimally to others and that their audiences appreciate them for exactly who they are. My experience over 30+ years is straight-forward in that most people:

a. Don't understand that they have a personal brand;

b. Don't spend any real time understanding themselves as a brand;

c. Have never taken the time to study all the factors that have influenced their brand from childhood to present day;

d. Struggle with the concept of writing down their strengths and weaknesses let alone even knowing their Achilles' heel or how to protect it;

e. Do not see themselves the way others see them;

f. Act inconsistently versus how they profess themselves and their brand to be;

g. Have varying degrees of emotional instability;

h. Have a Facebook page with indiscreet photos and private information that would shock their parents, professors or potential employers;

i. Have profoundly strong opinions about corporate ethics and integrity but see nothing wrong with pirating music and videos to download onto their I-Pod;

j. Hang out with people who deteriorate the value of their brand by contradicting the values they profess; and,

k. Are shocked when they get feedback from their professors, friends or their first boss that completely contradicts how they see themselves.

How's that for a mouthful? Is any of this ringing true with you? Be honest now because if you can't be honest with yourself then the core foundation of your brand is doomed. If you have not been dedicating any time to your own personal brand then it's time to begin. Your brand comes from within you and represents your core values and beliefs. The brand image you present publically cannot be something that you are intrinsically not. It must feel right and comfortable to you…like the warmth and touch of your own skin.

You will never be truly successful in life until you've learned how to be comfortable in your own skin. This is why you need to know, and like your own personal brand.

It took me years to fully comprehend the importance of this statement to my own personal brand. I'm sure I read it somewhere when I was younger but it didn't crack through my defensiveness. Until I started understanding myself better, I was anything but comfortable in my own skin. In fact, I was carrying on my daily existence in several suits of skin depending on the situation and the people with whom I was interacting. You mustn't try to act differently in front of various audiences. You must be one person at all time. I'd like to refer you to Addendum One for a three stage personal branding exercise. I think you will find this an invaluable tool. It looks very simple to complete but if you approach this with complete honesty and candor I think you'll find it quite an in-depth exercise to help you learn who you are; why you are that person; how your actions are (in)consistent with how you see yourself; and, what actions you need to take to become the best person you can be. Take a look at Addendum One and give it a fair shot.

Chapter 2 Highlight:

People who successfully brand themselves reap incredible rewards. Guarding the cornerstones and foundations of your brand is a full-time job. If you know that your target audiences are seeing you exactly how you wish to be seen, then you are on the right track to success. You will find life so much easier and fulfilling when you have found that heart-bolstering comfort in your own skin. You owe it to yourself to be the best person/ brand you can possibly be.

Chapter 3

Find the <u>right</u> job, not just a job

"Oh, so you hate your job? Why didn't you say so? There's a support group for that. It's called EVERYBODY, and they meet at the bar..."

-Drew Carey

When I address audiences of university students I begin with a simple question.

"Why are you here?"

I clarify that I'm not asking why they are sitting there listening to me speak rather than laying in bed catching up on some much needed shut-eye. I'm asking why they are at the university at all. I'm greeted by stunned expressions. Eventually answers get shouted out from behind the opened laptops.

"To learn. To meet girls. To party. To get a job. To get laid."

Always the same answers get shouted out at every school. Comfortably satisfied that they've answered my questions, the students sit back waiting for me to proceed but I just stand there and stare at them. Slowly, I repeat my question. The number of stunned and confused faces increases. Eventually, someone in that audience pipes up correctly.

"To find the job that's right for me."

Bingo.

University is not just about partying, hooking up and getting some sort of a degree that will get you a job. Think back to Chapter 1 and the playing field awaiting your graduation. If your attitude is simply to find any job then start practicing the phrase, "do you want fries with that sir?" You'll be able to practice that a lot as you continue to live at home with your parents.

If you are still a student then make a conscious decision to invest 50% more energy into your school than you currently are expending. **Your years in university are designed to help you: wean yourself from your home life; find your way socially with a whole new group of people; pick up a new tool box full of skills to help arm you for the working world; and most importantly, to learn about yourself and what it is you really should be doing in life.**

This last part seems to be missing in a lot of graduates and younger employees already in the workforce. There is no guarantee that your degree or diploma will in fact land you a job. And if it does, then is it the right job for you, your brand positioning and skill set? These are the questions that you need to be investigating while you are in university. If you have just graduated, it's still not too late to step back and make sure you've made the right decision about your career.

For years I've watched employees (in their mid to late 20's) struggling with this Catch-22. They rushed through university and got their degree. They weren't exactly sure what to do when they graduated so they bombarded various industries with resumes to see what stuck. Some used their parents' connections to open doors so that they could get a job while they figured out what they really wanted to be doing. What a horrible way to enter the workforce.

So to those of you still in university and college: complete Chapter 2's exercise on personal branding. Gather appropriate advisors to help you foster your thinking about various career options. Remember to not get caught up in geography and for goodness sakes, don't follow the path directed by your parents unless it's the right path for you to take... not the right one for them to have you take. I hope you've learned the difference in that bear-trap.

While you are still at school, get out into various industries and do your homework. Ask to meet the management in these companies and get to know exactly what they do. Spend quality time with the people in the Human Resources group. Their job is to match new talent with company staffing needs. They don't want to make a faulty hire. Go armed with insightful questions. Bring ideas that you've been judiciously considering for their company. I guarantee that with your digitally-mastered way of thinking, you will see things that they have not considered. Check out how they respond to someone with new ideas. Do they pick up the phone and call someone in a position of authority and say, "Hey, you've got to see what one of our candidates just brought in. It's brilliant." Or do they smile and check their watches to see how much time is left in your interview?

Ask how they indoctrinate newer, younger employees. Do they believe Gen Y'ers feel entitled and are they apprehensive about them? What is their game-plan to help various generations come together? How do they use Net Geners' expertise to help the company? When they hire people, are they utilizing social media vehicles?

Thoroughly investigate if one industry or company makes more sense to you than another. I'd be trying to understand which industries in various countries were going to offer the most growth and potential for employees. I'd want to comprehend international transfers and formalized training programs. **Don't take for granted that each company offers the same remuneration, benefits or medical coverage…because they don't.**

Keep clear records and refer back to the charts you completed in Chapter 2. Do the industries and the companies you are targeting match your goals and needs? Just how dramatically will you have to modify your personal brand and actions to meet the company brand and requirements?

Employ the internet to your advantage. Use your ingenuity and become a web-savvy Sherlock Holmes in relentlessly seeking out information. Your generation is famous for your ability to skate through the internet so use that ability for yourself. Rank (in writing) each company you target against the following factors that any employee should expect:

1. Integrity and honesty are the norm from the most senior to junior ranks. Any company worth its salt should be able to substantiate these are not mere words on a plaque in the lobby;

2. Employee safety is not limited to workers wearing hardhats and steel-toed boots. Employee safety includes people never feeling pressured because of their gender, age, race or religion. It means being in a location with emergency evacuation procedures and proper security for those working late at night;

3. Every employee needs to have a clearly written job description with timelines for salary and promotion reviews; action standards against which performance will be judged; an understanding of company policies (and how they are enforced); and formalized training that is integral to the employee's career plan;

4. Each employee must know that (s)he will be treated with respect by other employees, management, clients or suppliers;

5. **Fair pay is given for fair work done.** There will be times when overtime is required but most provinces and States have legislation to protect employees from being time-abused in their jobs;

6. Senior management communicates with the rank and file about the company's vision and business plan. Look for organizations that have an employee feedback mechanism so that the conversations are not just one way; and,

7. The company encourages new thinking, debating and better ways of doing business.

Don't take a job until you have answers to these factors or you will be talking with a Headhunter sooner than you should be.

I strongly urge you to grab a copy of Fortune February, 2010 and look at "The 100 Best Companies to work for!" The list was compiled by Milton Moskowitz, Robert Levering and Christopher Tkaczyk. Their #1 ranking went to SAS which at printing was the world's largest privately-owned software company. It boasts an employee turnover of 2% and as the writers noted, "has a laundry list of benefits including high-quality child care, 90% coverage of health insurance premium, unlimited sick days, a medical centre staffed by four physicians and 10 nurse practitioners (at no cost to the employees), a free 66,000 square-foot fitness center, a lending library, and a summer camp for children."

This is not your ordinary company and 95% of the companies out there won't be in their league. The point is that companies like this do exist and it's up to you to thoroughly seek out the right place for you to be. Try not to settle for second best.

Chapter 3 Highlight:

You will not be happy or fulfilled if your job does not match your personal brand and focus on your strongest skills. The hunt to determine and investigate your career begins long before your final term.

Throw your net far and wide and thoroughly investigate organizations to find a good match. Take nothing for granted and do not make assumptions. Net Geners are reputed to be incredible sleuths at pulling information from the computer. Doesn't your future deserve the same passionate intensity of investigation?

Chapter 4

Choreograph your career like a fine dance

"First comes the sweat. Then comes the beauty—if you are lucky enough and have said your prayers..."

-George Balanchine

You are just beginning your career. It seems that you are in a job that makes sense for you. The pay is reasonable. The company's medical plan has kicked in so you can finally go to the dentist. Your job is challenging and most days you leave feeling you have contributed to the team and learned something new. The company's computers are a bit of joke and there are days you sit at your desk contemplating life after university. Your responsibilities aren't overwhelming although you are being asked to work beyond normal hours. You've met a lot of people in the company: some interesting and others, well, not so interesting. As the weeks pass you start to wonder what the pathway for you is in the company.

In this chapter I'm going to talk about how you direct and "choreograph" your career pathway. Would you jump out of an airplane using a parachute you hadn't personally packed? Would you scuba dive alone down to 120 feet without proper training and certification? This chapter will help you understand that the overall orchestration of your career is up to you: not your parents, your professors or your supervisor. It's up to you.

From my first day on the job, I was schooled to look out for my own career. I actually set aside time each couple of weeks to step away from the game and ensure I was on track. With practice, it came easier for me to set milestones and target dates to check my own progress. Some companies for whom I worked spent a lot of energy in looking at their employees' career paths and how to best deploy them throughout the organization. My experience is that nowadays fewer companies have the resources, finances or inclination to make this effort. **You must never relinquish the choreographing of your career to anyone else.**

What does choreography look like?

How do the masters on 'So You Think You Can Dance," choreograph untrained dancers? Well, they uncover considerable raw talent and then they employ a lot of effort, experience, sweat and clear communication. They relentlessly practice the moves and try to match elements and flow of the dance with skills already possessed by the dancers. They carefully select music that will best show off their designed moves while stimulating the dancers to bring the music to life. A PR manager is brought in to help the dancer position themselves properly to their audiences and to the press. Eventually a business manager will be brought in to orchestrate the dancer's finances and investing. However, if a dancer cannot keep up to the requirements or doesn't garner the affections of the voting audience, they are voted off the show.

Why should your career be any different to a successful dancer? I'd like to set some frameworks based on the following:

A. Determining your leitmotifs

B. Choreographing begins with your personal brand

C. Finding your way around, or through a weak supervisor

D. How to confront an inept boss

E. Knowing when not to duck

F. Realizing when to cut bait and find a new job

A. <u>Determining your leitmotifs</u>

At the beginning of the book I shared the "5 guideposts" against which I decided to filter personal and career decisions. As the years progressed these "5" still seemed to apply and when I ignored them

I stumbled and made poor choices that hurt me. In due time, they became a part of my popular consciousness.

Every journey has to have a starting point against which you can judge your decisions and know when and how to course correct. Any choreographer has a basic dance in mind before (s)he begins the music. Here are the '5 leitmotifs' I determined were vital for me:

1. Never to be in a mind-numbing mundane job;
2. Never being in an isolated job but rather to be interacting with others of varying skill sets and generations;
3. Experience the world;
4. Be in a job where I could find more efficient ways of making things run; and,
5. Learn everything about being on, and leading winning teams.

I challenged you in the preface to understand your leitmotifs. If you honestly filled out Addendum One's charts, these should be pretty easy to document. Write them down and then relook them every couple of days for the next few weeks. Be very succinct and use some ingenuity. See if decisions you have already been making would have successfully passed these filters.

>**I will judge my choices and decisions against these leitmotifs:**

1.

2.

3.

4.

____

____

5.

____

____

If you have launched your career, how does your current job stack up against the 5 parameters you just wrote down? I'll wager 50% of you are rubbing their heads in disbelief that your current job isn't a match with what you think it should be. If you are one of them, then I'm glad you are reading this book.

B. <u>Choreographing begins with your personal brand</u>

This exercise is the choreographer selecting the dance after having culled down raw talent. Now let's discuss the music and the moves. When you start your career, you must go at it with eyes wide open. Leave any naivety at the door: this is not a practice or high school. This is real life and you will be held accountable for your actions and everything you say. If you want to be successful then learn to keep your trap shut. Do not be having "off the record" conversations about your boss with fellow employees. Do not pipe up with opinions that are not well-considered. My rule of thumb is the "10 second pause" standard: **if you have something to say, hold onto it for 10 seconds and consider the reaction to your words...before your lips move.**

Go at your new job as if your career depends on it...because it does. If reasonable overtime is required then do it without complaint. If the company is going through a rough time then be that special employee that comes forward with a new idea to drive the company or to build employee morale. Don't sit back and do what everyone is expecting of you. That's a dangerous thing to do when senior management's role is to keep salary costs in line. Go beyond your job description and prove to the company that they made an outstanding choice in hiring you. Ensure no one's gun-sights are set on you.

New employees will often complain that they are so busy to mundane tasks that they don't have time to go beyond the words in their job description. I tell them the issue is two-fold if they intend to succeed in their career. First, they have to become phenomenal time managers and get more done than the people with whom they are competing. Second, they have to learn how to logically say "no" to their bosses when too much is being put on their plate. It's your accountability to manage your time. **Until you learn to say "no," your boss will continue to load up your project list until you aren't able to give the right effort to the important tasks**. You will also lose any hope for having a balanced life.

So learn how to manage your time, say "no" and bring forward new thinking and ideas that surpass your written job description.

Now, how do you ensure that your personal brand is being properly appreciated, evaluated, recognized and rewarded?

1. Keep a list of every project and task on your plate including the over and above projects you wish to initiate;

2. Book a weekly update with your supervisor and share your list. Show how you are executing your projects and ask for input on how you could be doing them better or differently. Here's a little hint in life about tackling your projects: **I'd rather have a good idea beautifully executed than an outstanding idea poorly executed**;

3. Use these meetings to bring forward your new ideas that you and your boss should be tackling on the company's behalf; and,

4. Be open about asking for input and feedback on how things are going. Ensure that your target audiences are seeing you the way you want to be seen but don't come across as a needy employee requiring feedback every two seconds. Come across as an employee looking for the wisdom and expertise of someone more senior who can help guide their thinking and progress. Asking for regular feedback will also do two things: 1) uncover any issues your boss has before they are allowed to fester; and, 2) provide you with a temperature reading of just how positively your boss is viewing your contribution.

Arm your boss to help promote your career. Learn to do the dance and lead with grace. Never underestimate the critical importance of marketing yourself to the right people.

C. Finding your way around, or through a weak supervisor

What happens when you find yourself in the right job in the right company but with the wrong boss?

In my previous book, "A page from a CEOs Diary" I dedicated a chapter about interfacing and overcoming "bosses who are idiots." It's one of the chapters that garnered considerable feedback from readers who shared their own horror stories. Most of them survived the ordeal but not without having gone through incredible stress and episodes of total demoralization.

If you haven't already had an idiot boss, I guarantee you will. If you are still in school, this may be an "idiot professor" who believes the class average should be 65 and that doling out four hour assignments on Friday (due on Monday) is acceptable. The world is full of mentally-imbalanced fools who inexplicably snake their way into positions that can block you: Bosses whose attitudes and behaviors make you constantly feel anxious and focus more on your interaction with them than on the needs of your company. These troglodytes are nature's way of trying to dispel Darwin's theory of the fittest.

But here's a dubious glimmer of hope for you. Over my lifetime I have seen that eventually, monstrously-inept people get their comeuppance. There's a wonderful saying that I've seen attributed to philosophers in each of China, India and the Cherokee nation. It goes something along the lines that, "if you wait long enough on the banks of the river, you will watch the dead bodies of your enemies float by." I've been on those banks long enough to watch a good number of bodies floating by and it feels spectacular.

Here a statement I want you to meditate on.

Not all bosses are created equal and just because someone is more senior than you, doesn't make them better or smarter than you, or worth following. It's important for you to have mentors and experienced people who can help progress your career. Strive to work for people you admire and want to emulate.

Finding a really fabulous boss is not an easy task. You'll know you've got one when you can feel their efforts and determination to help you become the best person you can be. Once you find such a compassionate and charismatic leader...hang onto them as long as you can, because they are few and far between.

For the majority of your career, you will likely have average quality supervisors. Regardless of who is supervising you, never allow anyone with any title to ever disrespect you. **You can't be derided, disrespected or maltreated for any reason including your sex, the color of your skin, your religious beliefs, your nationality, or the size of your stomach.** Eleanor Roosevelt said, "People can only disrespect you if you allow them to." Most companies have policies on the fair treatment of their employees. In Canada and the USA, there are lawyers in the thousands who thrive on cases where employees have been mal-treated. The justice systems in both countries lean heavily to protect the employee's rights and fair treatment.

If you are being mal-treated or persecuted in your company, there are protocols and courses of action for you to pursue. It is not fair play that you are forced to quit your job and move on. Especially if you believe you are performing properly and have not been given adequate and fair feedback on performance issues. Why should you have to move on? Go to the company's HR department and investigate all pertinent company policies. If appropriate, seek legal counsel. Prepare yourself with information. Being a new employee is not grounds for being treated improperly.

Throughout my entire career, until now, I have entered every job with the underlying goal of taking my boss's job. I'm not saying that in a mean-spirited sort of way. I never had any intention of getting locked into, or left behind in one role or level. My approach was like a Panzer tank always moving forward. I realized from what I was witnessing in my first few years in the business world that there were several ways of achieving this goal.

1. **Get him/her promoted**: Help them look wonderfully successful at what they are doing so that their superiors tag them for a move up the ladder. I've had tremendous success being pulled up the corporate ladder handing onto the pant legs of a rising star. The trick was in identifying those "stars" and helping them realize that you could help drive their career

with your hard work, dedication, loyalty and political savvy. Machiavelli said, "Once you know a man's ambition, if you can assist him, he becomes beholden";

2. **Get him/her transferred**. This comes with several springboards of opportunity. Either help them look so good and diverse that the company seniors recognize how much more valuable your boss would be in a different capacity. Or, physically/visibly display how prepared you are for your boss's role while helping senior management realize that your boss is better suited for a different role. Not necessarily a more senior one;

3. **Get your boss fired**. I'm not going to elaborate on this one. I've never knowingly gone out of my way to get a boss fired. I always ask people the question "what are you prepared to do?" Well, this isn't one of those actions that I'm prepared to do. I think it's bad form, although I have watched it done with a peculiar fascination;

4. **Leapfrog your boss in the company**. I've done this three times in three different companies. The senior people in the company felt I displayed that I was a stronger longer-term employee with more upside potential. Those aren't my words… they are the words I was told each time. I felt awkward in each scenario but looking back realized that it was not an issue of fault or disloyalty. I had simply over-delivered and had won over management. I was always looking at new methodologies to improve the company's performance and efficiency. I tried to see what was coming at us from various directions. That mind-set just seemed to open up doors of opportunities and new ways of thinking. Paul Allen of Microsoft fame said, "In my own work, I've tried to anticipate what was coming over the horizon, to hasten its arrival, and to apply it to people's needs in a meaningful way."

   I will state for the record that in all three cases, I was extremely supportive of my supervisor and tried my best to look out for their careers;

5. **Get your boss demoted**. I imagine this is a real skill that I don't know that I have the mental prowess or dexterity to orchestrate. Given labor laws, I'm not sure it would be worth the potential severance; and,

6. **Get your boss out-placed**. Early in your career you need to build your street reputation with Placement Firms. Decide on 2-3 Head Hunters and get to know them. A really terrific recruiter can help you immensely in your current position by providing you information on what's happening in your company. They can let you know how your company is viewing you while earmarking any landmines you might be in the midst of stepping on. A good recruiter with whom you've formed a solid working relationship can be incredibly astute at spotting a stronger opportunity for you. And of course, a recruiter can bring alternate job opportunities to your boss.

What you must never do is to become content in one position. Silently suffering an idiot boss without speaking up is paramount to giving your unspoken consent to be misused or disrespected. Don't believe that there is some grand plan for you in the company's mind. 30+ years in business has proven to me that most companies view you as an expendable commodity that generates money. I know this sounds horribly callous and vulgar. Unfortunately, companies that give great attention to the longer-term career development of their employees tend to be the anomaly and are few and far between.

You must be vigilant about your career and shrewdly understand your role and interaction with your boss. This is a crucial game that will require a nimble mind, sharp foresight and careful footwork like dancing the fandango in the dark with a hippo. Don't be told that you're too young for a promotion or some specific assignment. Don't give 100% trust to your supervisor because you will never know their true intentions for you with regards to your career. There is always a way out of any ugly situation if you believe it's possible. As Hannibal, he of the elephants not of the Lector variety, is quoted as saying, "We will either find a way or make one."

D. How to confront an inept boss

Before you take on your painfully-inept boss, you need to make some very clear determinations about your company and your career. **Never enter a battle unless you understand the terrain; your opponent's strengths and weaknesses; and, how you will withdraw if that's required.** Before engaging in a confrontation with your boss you must have air-tight answers to the following:

1. Is this company worth working for if they negligently allow such gross incompetence in their senior people?

2. Can you get transferred to a position away from your current boss without getting a negative mark on your record?

3. **How long can you remain in the current position before your boss's inadequacies/reputation sully your reputation?**

4. How can you avoid a "boomerang" and prevent your boss from viciously blaming his/her shortcomings on your performance?

5. Is it possible for you to get around your boss to his/her supervisor and help them understand your contribution without stating the issues and dynamics you are encountering with your boss? You must not come across being disloyal to your supervisor. No matter how good you are, no one else will trust you if they see you debasing a more senior person.

6. Work harder to deliver your role which is an astute way of catching the attention of other senior people.

It's not easy having an idiot boss yet it will probably happen to you more than once in your career. It's a real learning experience and I guarantee that if you approach it professionally and wisely, it will make you immeasurably stronger. While you are trying to move beyond this situation you should be preparing yourself to be able to secure a position in another company.

I would ask that you reflect upon your own developing supervisory skills and ensure that your own reports aren't viewing your leadership as being inadequate.

Taking a stand with your boss when your career has just begun

Here are some suggestions on how to stand up and not be crucified:

> have a discussion with the Human Resources or Personnel departments explaining your situation; your frustration; and, your past attempts to remedy the situation;

> document everything you discuss with the HR department;

> meet privately with your boss during working hours;

> close the door to ensure your conversation is not overheard;

> be prepared to listen in the event that there is more to the situation than you know;

> **never show emotions and do nothing rash, or spur of the moment;**

> do not confront in an e-mail or a phone recorded message;

> do not raise your voice no matter how loud your boss gets;

> be prepared to back up your words by having the matter taken to your boss's supervisor. Don't engage in a confrontation until you have firmly decided what you are prepared to do if it goes ugly;

> have your ducks in order to go to his/her supervisor with: proper written documentation of things your boss has said about his supervisor; and, names of people in the company who are aware of your boss's shortcomings as well as your contribution to the company; and,

> immediately document, date and sign everything that is said by both parties and keep a copy in your home files. This will prove helpful if the matter goes the legal route.

You will encounter confrontations with your boss in the normal conduct of your job. Knowing when and how to take a stand throughout your career can be manifested in many ways.

E. Learning when not to duck

You are going to run into an abundance of problems throughout your life: some of your own making and others that you had nothing to do with. The issues that pop up and try to derail your career won't always be fair...but who promised you that life was supposed to be fair? Here's a story I guarantee will become relevant to you in your future.

You are 23-25 years old and have just been promoted to a supervisory role. Through no fault of your own, a younger, less experienced employee you supervise (Ying Wang) completely screws up a project. You had kept close track of the project and had made yourself available whenever you were needed. Your directions and expectations were judicious and abundantly crystal clear. You had set very enthusiastic deadlines and scheduled milestone meeting updates every week. While it would seem improbable for any project to go off track, the inconceivable has happened and Ying Wang is standing in front of you in tears. In-between intermittent sobs, Ying tells you that in order to save time she made assumptions about a critical piece of information: assumptions that she just discovered were erroneous. The company has been compromised and when the proverbial S**T hits the fan you and Ying are not going to get any sympathy for your plight.

As calmly as you can, you determine the gravity of the problem and ascertain actions to get the project on track. You pull together new timelines and potential cost overages. In order to be completely transparent, you immediately e-mail your supervisor (Meredith Bouillot) and share the situation and how you are handling it. You clearly document the potential financial risk at hand and admit the timeline is in danger. You ask for your boss's counsel and ask how she would like to inform senior management. Meredith responds to your e-mail with a curt reply of concern and disappointment. Her message is unmistakably articulate. "Fix the damned problem right now. Who is to blame for this incompetence?"

With adrenalin surging like a geyser, you personally step in and work 24/7 to rectify the problem and resuscitate the project. Despite the Herculean effort of you and your team, the deadline is missed and the firm takes a severe financial hit. Not unexpectedly, you are summoned to Meredith's office for a meeting.

"Close the door and sit down," a haggard and worn-looking Meredith Bouillot orders, as she paces back and forth in front of her desk. She turns and stares suspiciously at you with fierce blue eyes. You feel anxious and involuntarily begin to sweat.

"I just got off the phone with Richard who is absolutely furious over this catastrophe. (Richard MacAllister is Meredith's boss and the Division VP). We're going to miss next quarter's revenue targets. He just ripped me a new one and wants to know what I'm going to do about this."

Your formidable boss is seething mad and out for blood. Her face and neck are crimson and blotchy and she is gritting her teeth. You notice that she is no longer making direct eye contact with you. She has a penchant for being dramatic and a well-documented inclination to fire quickly.

How do you read this precarious situation? From what you've experienced in this company, is Meredith's job on the line? Is yours? You informed her by e-mail and suggested she update her superiors. Is Richard is so irate because Meredith didn't inform him? This potential communication failure by Meredith is a critical piece of data. The next few minutes could prove deadly to Ying Wang's career...and possibly your own.

"So what the hell happened?" Meredith launches at you in a tirade like an avalanche exploding down a mountain. "I want to know who is to blame for this mess and I want them fired today. Are you to blame for this? Should I be firing you? Tell me why I shouldn't fire you? Start talking!"

Your tormentor is standing 3 feet away from you and she isn't role-playing. There won't be any video rewind or Mulligan on this one.

This is a case of career choreography.

Your boss has never displayed this kind of fury in your presence. Do you extricate yourself by fingering your employee? It was Ying's fault for having made an erroneous assumption and then misleading you. In all fairness, this releases you from accountability and blame. You fixed the problem as far as you could and without your efforts the financial hit the company took would have been astronomically worse. Besides, Ying Wang is young, smart and can find a new job quickly. This would be a good lesson for her and definitely a character builder.

The silence is the room has become deafening except for the sound of a pounding heart in your eardrums. So what would you do in such a compromising situation?

I have seen this exact situation no less than 6 occasions. At least half of those times, I witnessed supervisors throw their employee under the bus faster than the astonishing speed with which Kanye West unabashedly grabbed the microphone from an unsuspecting and bewildered Taylor Swift.

I have also witnessed bosses defiantly shielding their team members from harm: voluntarily accepting full accountability and whatever punishment came along with it. That's the action of a true leader: to stand firm; explain the details of what happened; outline how the situation has been remedied; and clearly lay out how the problem will never be repeated. It is to demonstrate how you have managed the situation back on track and how your team is aware of what happened. You need to graciously apologize for not having caught the issue earlier. The words, "I'm sorry and this will never happen again" must come out of your mouth. And they'd better be sincere.

Here's the ultimate crux of it.

You have the accountability for the entire project. Your team members do not. They have the responsibility which you have placed upon them...but you are accountable and should have ensured that Ying Wang was better supervised. The fact that you gave up the overall accountability was monstrously unprofessional. It is your accountability to ensure your team is only ever dealing with facts. Assumptions will sink you faster than the loathsome iceberg that killed the Titanic. Why did you only e-mail Meredith? When you are in trouble, e-mail is only one form of communication. It's time for face to face long before the deadline is up. I hope that you are always clever enough to keep your boss (and his/her boss) informed and up to date on your projects. Don't conceal problems when they occur. Your supervisor(s) may be able to help if you bring him/her in early enough.

The act of a true leader is to ensure that any repercussions to your team are yours to accept. Have the courage to stand up, ferociously protect your employees, stick out your chin and take the hit…even if it means being demoted or losing your job.

If your supervisors or fellow employees ever see you protect yourself by forsaking and deserting one of your employees you will pay for it. I would refer to this as a pyrrhic victory. King Pyrrhus of Epirus battled the Romans in 280 B.C. and suffered crippling losses while defeating his enemy in two key battles. The Romans had even greater casualties but unlike Pyrrhus, were able to return with fresh troops. Pyrrhus' victory was short lived because it came with devastating costs. So will yours be if you ever knowingly and unjustly toss an employee to the wolves.

Over years of being in supervisory roles, I have had a number of my own staff members screw up even when I was carefully watching. Some of those mistakes were honest and innocent; some were from reckless expediency; some were out of laziness; and some were from downright stupidity. I can proudly state that I never threw anyone under the bus. I stood my ground and refused to duck. The outcomes served me well:

>I have been reprimanded, balled out and screamed at...but never career-damaged for standing up for my employees;

>I have been rewarded by management for my display of leadership to my team and honesty to the company;

>The loyalty of my reports increased ten-fold; and,

>Other employees witnessed my loyalty and asked to work for me.

To those who haven't learned about when to take a hit: listen up. You will never be your best if you bob and weave your way out of every fight. Find inside you a surge of courage, contemplate the gravity of the situation and demonstrate you understand the mantle of command. Learn when and how to stand up and take a punch even though it would be easier to duck.

F. Realizing when to cut bait and find a new job

This is a discussion point that gets posed to me at least once a week.

It is time to leave your current company when:

1. You realize your company is dealing unethically with its employees, clients, customers or suppliers. Perhaps they are knowingly selling a faulty or unsafe product or service. You may decide to "whistle blow" to more senior ranks or the authorities. Either way, it's time to go;

2. Your CEO and/or CFO are taken out of their offices in hand-cuffs. Make sure your ducks are in order; and, get your resume on the street;

3. Your boss/supervisor refuses to treat you with proper respect

and dignity and your pleas for assistance and intervention are ignored;

4. A Head-Hunter's phone call keeps you awake that night and you realize you haven't been that excited about an opportunity in years;

5. An opportunity arises to work for a former boss who you believe is the best boss you ever had and you can't think of any reasons not to take the job;

6. Supervisors keep telling you that 'the time just isn't right' every time you attempt to improve your current position and salary;

7. You dread getting up for work 50% of the time;

8. Most of your day is spent day-dreaming about something else you'd rather be doing or surfing the web; and,

9. You start considering ways of taking financial advantage of your company to make up for how little they are paying you (i.e. playing hooky and claiming sick days/stealing computer equipment).

You are not chained to your current job and it's up to you to logically decide whether to remain or find a new job. It's all too easy to stay in an unhappy job or situation because of the unknown territory you will find yourself in if you make a switch. Adlai Stevenson said, "Change is inevitable. Change for the better is a full-time job."

Chapter 4 Highlight:

You are accountable for your own life and career: not your parents, friends, professors or boss. If you don't take control of events, they will either take control of you, or pass you by. You'll find yourself looking in the mirror at the age of 40 wondering what happened.

Your career is like an exciting, fine dance that requires preparation, practice and the right song. Take control of how you are making decisions and just what you are prepared to do.

Chapter 5

Set your quality bar for 'excellence'

"We are what we repeatedly do. Excellence then is not an act, but a habit..."

-Aristotle

It was easy standing behind that toothpick chopper watching the blades do their job: brain cell deteriorating but easy. The employees on the choppers had to deliver a certain hourly quota of flats filled with toothpicks, medical tongue depressors or swizzle sticks. So when one case was filled, you had to shut down your machine and do a quality control. There would be a second quality control after the products had dried out and were being packed for shipping. This chapter is going to address how you envision quality control in your life and embody excellence in your thoughts and actions.

My supervisor at Kennans was a meticulous QC checker. Jo Walker had been with Keenans for thirty years and explained to me the importance of catching faulty products and never relying on someone else at a later stage in the manufacturing process.

"How would you like to be a customer and open up one of our boxes of toothpicks and find some broken, or poorly made?" Jo asked theoretically, as we sorted through the wooden products and removed broken, burnt or misshaped toothpicks.

Now frankly, even as Jo was telling me this I wasn't sure I would have given the quality of a toothpick a second thought. It's not like finding a problem with your car or something important. It was only a two dollar box of toothpicks for God's sake.

Jo Walker went on to explain about the importance of the company's name and reputation and how jobs were protected when our customers felt they were getting the top product at a good value. She told me the outcome of a quality misstep could be catastrophic for everyone in the factory. I thought a lot about this as I inspected my output. It hadn't dawned on me that jobs could be affected by poor product quality. I always assumed that there was someone else who would catch and fix issues. **Never assume anything in life.**

I started investing more time inspecting the quality of my work which got encouraging nods of approval by the more seasoned employees. It finally dawned on me that it didn't matter if a customer opened up a box of Keenan's toothpicks and marveled at how wonderful the products were. What truly mattered was the customer finding poor product quality and then complaining to the store at which they were purchased. Now you have two customers angry with you: the distributor and the customer. That's when sales can be cut, the faulty product being purchased back by the factory and subsequently jobs lost.

This monumentally critical lesson about quality control on something as basic and mundane as a toothpick served me well in university and when I started working in the real world. It's often paying attention to the smallest details that helps you succeed on much bigger projects. I've learned a little rule of thumb that makes some people laugh when they hear it. Before I hire someone, I check the heels of their shoes, regardless of whether they are male or female. If I see that the heels are worn down and uncared for it gives me an indication that the candidate doesn't look to the details in their lives. And if they are willing to let little things go for themselves then what will they bring to little things that are important to my company?

Have you noticed how often people seem prepared to settle for delivering a product or service that's just "good enough?" Perhaps you've heard the phrase, "good is the enemy of great." I want you to know that good just isn't good enough. It's a weakness in attitude and character. **Great results will only be achieved when you understand**

the importance of an excellent effort/result and then refuse to settle for any lesser outcome.

What makes the difference between a student who gets a 'B' grade and a student who gets an 'A' grade? What differentiates the Olympic sprinter who painstakingly crosses the finish line .005 seconds ahead of the second place finisher: the loser whose name will only be remembered by his family and friends? Was it preparation? Luck? Genes? Coaching? Did the sprinter have a greater desire to win from beginning to end? Did the student simply study harder?

What makes a winner a winner?

We've all come across people with average IQs from average backgrounds who have shown ingenious sparks of greatness in various endeavors in their lives. These people excelled to the highest ranks in their chosen fields of business, sports, medicine, music or entertainment. I've always considered that there is a great deal of luck, time and place that helps some people succeed where others fail. However, I have observed an unquestionable common thread to winners which goes much deeper than just time and place. **The common thread to winners is an unyielding, indefatigable quest for excellence.**

Vince Lombardi, famed coach of the Green Bay Packers was quoted as saying, "The quality of a person's life is in direct proportion to their commitment to excellence, regardless of their chosen field."

Do you religiously strive to deliver your best results every time? Are you content to live in a digital world of headlines or will you vigilantly go deeper and understand what's beneath the surface so you can best arm yourself with facts and knowledge? Almost as important, are you surrounding yourself with people who strive to deliver excellence?

How about a reality check?

Let's be realistic. We are all rushed frantically in an electronic quagmire-like world where cell phones, Blackberries, professors, bosses, parents and significant others can metaphorically speaking, "suck the living breath out of us." I get it. You won't be able to nail every task every time. Comprehending that is important but adopting that as an ongoing excuse is not acceptable. That's how you will become the proverbial "B" student or the person who always finishes in second place. Besides, don't you feel like you've compromised yourself and your integrity when you allow outside influences to hamstring your best effort? I know I feel intractable anxiety, and the demoralizing guilt that was ingrained in my Catholic upbringing comes back to torment me.

Understand you won't always be on your game. The dictates of life will constantly pull at you and try to distract and hamper you from being your best day in and day out. That's okay. Now, as you approach a task or job, stop and determine whether this is one of those times. What happens to you, your career, your health and your family if you only deliver an average output on the specific task facing you? Will you fail the grade? Could you lose your job? Conversely, what happens if you unequivocally ace the task? Who is watching? How will your work be viewed, used and implemented? How will this come back on you positively, or negatively?

Let's proceed on the basis that you are approaching a task or job that you've determined is absolutely vital to your success: your job may depend on it. What are guidelines to improve your odds of superior success?

First, envision and define the objective of your task in multiple ways. This is not about meeting a deadline. **It's about meeting the deadline with the best effort, unequalled thinking and irrefutable results you can muster.** A three-legged monkey can meet a deadline. Go at this task with an unsympathetic eye and fastidiously analyze it from all dimensions. Do you fully understand the task, the intricacies of the issues, the deliverables, the timing, the budget, the audience, the inherent risks, the potential roadblocks and the outcomes? Do you really understand the game behind the task you are attacking?

Marcus Aurelius was a leader and visionary of great distinction. Aurelius was the Roman Emperor from 161-180 A.D. and was considered the last of the five great emperors. An ingenious strategist, Marcus Aurelius also wrote a book called Meditations. An immaculate philosopher, he said, "The wise man sees in the misfortunes of others what he must avoid." His burning desire to achieve military and historic excellence led the Roman Empire to conquer all of Europe.

As a kid, did future Olympian speedster Usain Bolt stroll out from his parents' grocery store in Trelawny, Jamaica and profess that when he was 22 years old he would win 3 Olympic Gold medals for the 100m,

200m and 4x100m relay races? Of course he didn't. He probably went outside and played tag or soccer to avoid doing his homework. However, as he got older, he and others obviously realized his potential as a world-class runner. Bolt began training and studying his craft. He meticulously learned from other champions' mistakes and failures. Usain Bolt never relented in his desire to become the fastest man on the planet.

Although, Bolt arrived on the planet over 1,800 years after Marcus Aurelius ruled the Roman world, the Jamaican sprinter had this same unyielding desire for excellence. Through relentless training and a unswerving heart of persistence he overcame anything blocking his way to shattering world records and bringing home the gold.

We've had a shining example of reaching for the stars arrive on the scene over the past 2 years in the most recent Presidential race. Whether Democrat or Republican you must admit that Barrack Obama's race to the White House was a beautifully orchestrated and executed strategy of astonishing excellence. Did Barrack Obama come to the astonishing declaration as a teenager that running for the leadership of the Democratic Party was his only course in life? Did he fully comprehend the glacial odds against him seeking and running for the Presidency of the United States of America? At some point in his life, Barrack Obama looked at the task facing him and decided it was worth pursuing with everything he had to give. He defined the task and methodically set out to improve his odds. With help, he created a very appealing personal brand. He surrounded himself with people of equal or superior talent. He analyzed his playing field and then orchestrated a roadmap to the White House while engaging a team of like-minded supporters. They strategized messaging, target groups, and what obstacles would await them. Obama continued to bolster his skill set and stayed the course until his timeline was achieved and his results were unquestionably excellent. The foundations of how I see him tackling this quest included:

1. Looking abstractly outside the accepted political rulebook on how, where and when to campaign and spend campaign dollars;

2. Taping into the popular consciousness of a country desperately looking to rejuvenate their belief in themselves;

3. Eliciting tremendous moral support and a tidal wave of financial contributions using the old-fashioned "door to door canvassing" in 2008 terms using the internet; and,

4. Holding to his principles for excellence and refusing to be distracted, or dragged down into the mire by his pugnacious antagonists.

Preparing yourself for a task requires you first to decide just what you are prepared to do. Then, taking a page from Obama, you need substantial help and considerable support to pull it off.

No man, or woman is an island:
amass a great team around you

As you are determining your game-plan, step back and think about the skills you will need to bring together to complete the job. Your team-mates shouldn't always be the same faces because different issues require different skill sets. Don't feel that because you are in a junior role that you don't have people and advocates you can add to your team. Of course you do. Your team may be comprised of your boss, other co-workers, students, family members, clients or suppliers. Forming a really strong legitimate support group is like having a safety net under the high wire. You need others' expertise, involvement, feedback and quality control. **Turn your spirit of collaboration into an art form.**

Let's talk more specifically about your team and the people with whom you work. The faster you learn these lessons, the more successful you will be in your career and in any relationships you have.

Where your career is concerned here are some considerations on how to select and interact with your team-mates:

1. Take great care in whom you place your trust. Understand the intent behind any statements made to you professionally or personally.

2. **Be very selective in considering team-mates: don't conduct a popularity or good looks contest.** This is about bringing diversity, legitimate talents and charismatic thinking to your table. Age, ethnicity and gender on your team should reflect societal norms. If you want to out-leap your competition, build

a team of international scope reaching into universities for like-minded talents. In retrospect, my teams were always too "locally focused" and far too similar in background to my own.

3. If you are already in the workforce, some of your team-mates should not work in your company. Look back into your university or college and consider with whom you'd like to maintain a career relationship. Look to people who share common values and goals but have distinctly different skill sets than your own.

4. Don't make statements to your team about other people or your company that you wouldn't want aired on CNN. If you have nothing positive to say then keep your mouth shut. If people are thinking you are an idiot, don't open your mouth and prove them right. Contemplate the gravity of your words before they pass your lips.

5. Don't gossip to your team…but listen to gossip. Don't show your feelings or react without consideration. Uncontrolled gossip is a perilous undertaking and can euthanize the morale and equilibrium of any organization, including schools.

6. Your intelligence is not going to be enough to protect you. You need to use common sense and keep your eyes open for your own benefit and to protect your team. Be careful not to be dragged into any office politics by your team-mates.

7. Observe before engaging with your team. Don't dive into a lake before you know if there is a dead-head or rock hidden below the surface. Office politics are often like that submerged log lurking dangerously just out of sight. Encourage your team members to anticipate obstacles from the least likely sources.

8. Keep close to your team with face to face meetings and clear communication. Document everything. Don't allow any room for your team-members to misunderstand their accountabilities or deliverables. Every person should know exactly what their role is to achieve an excellent result. When one of your team members is not delivering it is up to you to sit down with

them and let them know. Do not entrust this to anyone else. Make everyone responsible for their piece of the puzzle but you maintain the accountability at all times.

There is always one more thing to do

Now that you have your team/support group in place and you've set a proper timeline with dated milestones, how will you know if you are proceeding properly? For this, you must set action standards and quality controls on the deliverables before any actual work begins. Schedule regular face to face check-in points with your professor (or supervisor). Keep them abreast of your progress and get their input along the way. This may pre-empt a big surprise later when you've strayed off course as we saw in my earlier story about Ying Wang and Meredith Bouillot. Always deliver exactly what you've been tasked to do and then deliver more: perhaps a slight twist in the objective; an alternative outcome; or a different take on how to use the results.

When you think your job or task is completed, take time to sleep on what you've done and consider the intangibles. I always try to build in a protective buffer to let my mind have a chance to visualize that "one more thing" that can take my output to a new level of excellence. I gather input and peculiar opinions from stakeholders who may see something that I've been just too close, or stubborn to recognize.

Don't allow Blackberries or the urgency of your professor, boss, or clients to prevent you from finding that one more thing to do. This "one more thing" is often the difference that makes the quality of your output excellent and not just good.

Chapter 5 Highlight:

Approach each task you undertake with a keen eye as to what effect it could have on your future. If it's a vital task then you must invest yourself fully in it to achieve an excellent outcome. Consider the project from all angles and then bring together the best resources and team members you can muster. Understand the deliverables and never give up the accountability of leadership. Remember that winners persist when obstacles arise. When you think you are done a job/task, step back and quality inspect your work.

There is always one more thing that you can do to make your product and output superior.

Chapter 6

Present an optimal attitude

"I was the kind nobody thought could make it. I had a funny Boston accent. I couldn't pronounce my R's. I wasn't a beauty..."

-Barbara Walters

People don't tend to appreciate having their attitude questioned and their immediate inclination is either to stop listening or argue vociferously. I hope you won't stop reading because the intent of this chapter to talk about your generation's supposed attitude problems. It's important for you to know what's awaiting you in the working world. This chapter is going to challenge you to reaffirm that your attitude is optimally supporting your personal brand.

In his book, 'grown up digital,' author Don Tapscott helps us learn about you, your inherent computer skills, your instinctive upbringing with the internet, your multi-tasking wizardry and how, if nurtured, you can bring an incredibly strong collaborative effort to the team. But Mr. Tapscott also writes, "you'll hear lots of older employers voice the same complaint: Young workers today are spoiled brats. They're making ridiculous demands of their employers, and they haven't even proven themselves. That feeling may be widespread."

So which is it and why are so many senior people concerned about what you will be bringing to the table?

1. Entitlement is such a turnoff

There are many books and articles that talk negatively about your generation's sense of entitlement: but one title sums it up. It's a book by Jean Twenge called, "Generation Me: Why Young Americans Are More Confident, Assertive, Entitled and More Miserable Than Ever Before." As a CEO, I often said that this new Digital Generation is a series of peculiar contradictions between attitude and actions. Net Geners' and the three words "sense of entitlement" almost always appear concurrently.

Do you feel entitled in life? I'd be surprised if you don't. How couldn't your generation help being spoiled when they had parties for doing everything from graduating Grade One to coming in tenth place in a track and field event. Our children got ribbons for being on the losing team. In Grade 4 our daughter was presented a bright red ribbon for finishing a race. I couldn't believe my eyes. The damned ribbon read, "Congratulations for coming in 8th."

Unfortunately for you, this anticipated sense of entitlement is a turnoff for the rest of us. It's important for you to know that the generations awaiting you are really concerned about this attitude. If in fact, you do fall into this "entitled" category you need to check your ego at the door to avoid crippling your career. If you aren't one of the "entitled" Net Geners then you must recognize that the awaiting generations may attribute this irreverent attitude to you until you prove otherwise.

This confounding issue is now in the popular consciousness of our society. I've had many discussions with fellow CEO's, clients, professors and friends about how outright spoiled your generation seems to be. When I look at resumes I see little that impresses me: few background or "summer jobs" sections. I know it was centuries ago, but when I entered the workforce, my resume showed a string of summer jobs that include manual labor and office work. I could talk about how I had budgeted and scrimped to make it through school. Part of the fun of the interview was sharing how I managed to uncover and secure some of those jobs. I took great pride in being able to say I put myself through school. Of course my parents helped out the best they could and I'm grateful for that. But the resumes I see today show summer camps, travel, and summer courses in Italy and France. For the most part, they are lacking in character building jobs that helped pay the school tab.

I spoke at a university a short time ago and was shocked to see every second student parading around a Blackberry and Smart Phone. As I drove onto the campus I was overwhelmed to see so many students driving brand new vehicles. During my speech, I asked a group of first year university students how many had paid for their own phones and the computers. Very few of the six hundred students raised their hands. I don't know if they were surprised by the indiscretion of my question or that I might even consider that perhaps they should be forking out the cost…or doing without.

How could you not feel entitled when it's been voluntarily bred into you? If idyllic parents reward a child for not doing their best then how will the child ever learn to do their best? How will younger persons learn to experience and overcome failure and defeat if Mom and Dad are always there to block out any hardships?

It is mind boggling how the people trying to help you have actually been retarding your development by systematically removing any hardships or strains along your journey. **I've come to know that it is exactly those hardships and strains that toughen your skin to the bad weather that awaits you in life.** I may have hated making toothpicks but there was a feeling of delicious fatigue at the end of every exhausting week when I counted the money I was putting away for school or something I wanted to buy.

I hope you will utilize the amazing qualities that define your generation. The world needs your technical expertise and collaborative spirit. We need your way of coming at issues in manners that are foreign to us. Governments may not like it but they need your ability to speak out through the internet when you witness political and social injustices. Companies are looking at your consumer base's interaction through social marketing with eyes filled both with greed and extreme trepidation should you take umbrage with their products.

Focus on using these wonderful qualities but leave any sense of entitlement at home.

2. Arrogance comes in all sizes

Let me share a story about a different expression of entitlement which is just as damaging. Arrogance is that attitude or expectation that you are better than someone else, more capable, more intelligent or more "knowing." Most arrogant people don't live up to their attitude and have detractors lined up trying to help them fail.

When I was first appointed CEO, my then-boss, Peter Stringham, Global CEO of Young & Rubicam in New York gave me some advice I wish I had heard when I was first entering my career.

"On any given day," Peter counseled, "You will bounce between being paranoid and arrogant numerous times. It's perfectly natural so don't try to fight it. Just don't allow yourself to be become overwhelmed with paranoia or arrogance."

As a leader you have so much information flying your way that it's almost impossible to find your right stride. Just when you think you've got the world by the tail, something comes out of left field and knocks you to the ground. You struggle, get up and find your way out of the mess. Things get back on track. Your confidence builds, you marvel at your skills and for a couple of days you can do no wrong. You learn from the incident and try to put in place fail-safes to prevent a repeat occurrence.

"God, I'm good," you boast in self-gratifying delight. "I am one heck of a marvelous CEO. This really isn't all that hard when you put your mind to it."

For a while everything goes according to Hoyle. You do better than Barrack Obama at an Illinois Democratic Fundraiser hosted by Bill Clinton with Bono and Lady Gaga providing the entertainment. Then completely out of the blue you get smacked again. This time from right field and even harder than the previous surprise. The arrogance and wind that was filling your sails gets sucked dry in a nanosecond like Tom Cruise's credibility when he unabashedly danced on Oprah's sofa, foolishly professing his love for Katie Holmes.

The routine carries on. You remedy the issue and catch your breath. You get hit again and knocked off your heels. As Peter advised, this teeter-totter doesn't necessarily wait for days to reverse course. I've been flipped for loops between arrogance and paranoia 2-3 times in one day. You start forming a schizophrenic personality and become scornfully jaded.

As the years have flown by, my CEO tenure has toughened my skin as successes and surprises try to flip me back and forth. With time, my arrogance has been so beaten down and my paranoia has been proven unnecessary that the teeter-totter doesn't swing too high, or too low. I've been able to find a more even keel with each grey hair and wrinkle. If I had only known thirty years ago, what I have had beaten in me by this stage in my career. I'm embarrassed when I think of how arrogantly I approached work situations when there was no call for it. Perhaps it was insecurity or naivety.

That's why I'm sharing this with you. I expect that with your youth and technical savvy you will have an element of arrogance: you have a lot to be proud of. It's about finding that balance of your arrogance with the real world and people who may not be willing to cut you an ounce of slack while you're getting your career started.

Before you are told you have an attitude problem, consider a course correction now. I find it helps to step out of my own skin for a while and refocus myself on those things most precious in my life: my health and my family. Once I re-center myself, my attitude settles down and I can go back at any issue with renewed vigor and spirit. Look back to Addendum One and how you completed it. What role does arrogance play in your personal brand?

As you enter the workforce and shift into different stages of your life, there will be "equalizers" that come along to help you get more rooted and balance your arrogance and humility. The arrival of our children proved to be one of the greatest equalizers that came into my world and helped burn out some of my own sense of entitlement and arrogance. It's hard not to taste humble pie when your children nail you from every orifice of their tiny bodies…any time of the day. I think my last shred of arrogance was burned out of me on a trip to Chicago. That was the day my darling five year old son threw up in my bare hands in the business section of an Air Canada plane as we were taking off. As I sat their squirming and trying not to throw up, I could only look at my boy's green face, the contents of my hands and look around at our fellow passengers.

"Lime Gatorade," was all I could mutter through gritted teeth. Tell me how anyone could feign any shred of arrogance after that.

3. The role of persistence in your attitude

So what should your attitude be since I'm telling you to cut out any elements of entitlement, arrogance and paranoia? How about balanced confidence and humility? How about using that collaborative spirit for which your generation is famous? How about an unyielding sense of curiosity and the willingness to speak up when you see something wrong? How about strengthening your beliefs in what you understand to be right and wrong?

From what I've observed, most people don't understand the importance of, and role that persistence plays in defining their brand and success. It seems that with the first hint of opposition, most people are ready and willing to back down from their objective. Does this mean that they aren't certain that their objective is correct, or that it is correct but not worth defending? The better objectives I've pursued in my career have always been met with opposition and near insurmountable obstacles. The easier objectives I selected were not met with any roadblocks…nor did they generate the level of outcome I had anticipated and hoped for.

One of the USA's more successful presidents was a very unassuming politician named Calvin Coolidge. He was a very solid leader who chose his words with extreme caution after considerable deliberation. This quote is attributed to Coolidge and it's one that I pull out and read every time I find myself under siege or facing what seems to be insurmountable obstacles.

"Nothing in this world can take the place of persistence. Talent will not; nothing is more common than unsuccessful people with talent. Genius will not; unrewarded genius is almost a proverb. Education will not; the world is full of educated derelicts. Persistence and determination alone are omnipotent."

When you graduate from university, you are going to encounter people who will represent different varieties of persistence. Recognizing which form of persistence you are encountering will afford you to orchestrate your involvement and interaction accordingly. You should also be considering which of these categories best describes you today and if you're happy about it.

*The **Army General** who will achieve his orders at any cost to himself or anyone else. The General expects everyone to obey his directives: ours is not to question why...ours is but to do or die. This is a very dangerous form of persistence. Unless you find yourself holding an M16 I suggest you limit your use of this approach to persistence and be very careful aligning yourself with any Army Generals. No one likes to be dictated to and people around you won't want to feel like casualties every time they try to support you.

*The **Reluctant Bride** will persist in getting to the altar on time but complain to everyone with each delay or obstacle. She has the horrible habit of making lives miserable while working towards her goal. The Reluctant Bride constantly questions herself and her decision to get married. She has her entourage wasting precious time reassuring her and trying to encourage her that her decision is correct. Your team-mates should not have to be your constant pillars of support and enthusiasm. Your resolve should be firm enough that it breeds confidence in those around you.

*The **Red Light/Green Light game-player** who charges into his objective rallying his supporters to his side only to stall and change directions towards a second, totally unrelated objective. Don't engage people unless you are focused on your course of action. Your course might not have the odd detour but shouldn't be running parallel with other ghost courses of action that distract you, and your supporters, from your goal.

*The **Mr. Persistence As Long As It Doesn't Get Ugly** is a very strong-willed personality who comes forth with an excellent, well-conceived objective with a reasonable timeline and a set of expectations. A team moves into support him. And then someone in a more senior role steps forward and raises concerns and Mr. PALAIDGU freezes like Chris Brown when asked by a reporter why he hit Rihanna. What typically happens is that the individual backs down and must retrench, refocus and try to get around the opposition. Fear for career enters the game and since it might go ugly, the individual decides not to persist in his endeavor. His team is left standing in the cold wondering why they wasted so much time.

*The **World Saving Zealot** is one of the more frustrating people to be around. Every cause that ever comes across their plate becomes a rallying cry to show their absolute love of humanity in a relentless manner that drives normal people crazy. If you don't engage with their cause you are nothing short of being a Nazi. Their persistence in rallying behind each cause becomes so overwhelming that they lose sight of what it is they are actually trying to achieve.

Let me share an example about a "World Saving Zealot" named Victoria: an extremely caring individual who is always involved in no less than five charities.

Last year, Victoria was focused on feeding the homeless in Toronto. She orchestrated a gathering of like-thinking people at 'Far Niente,' a very posh restaurant in the banking district. As we arrived, I saw the Vera Wang clad Victoria and two of her guests pass two homeless people asking for money. No one gave them a red cent. As we settled at our table, I suggested that perhaps we should agree to meet in a less expensive setting and then donate the money we would have spent on lunch to help the two homeless people standing on the street outside the restaurant. The reaction to my comment was swift and cutting.

"Howard, this is about amassing wider support and funding…not just for any two people standing around on the street."

The owner of that comment was Victoria: a definite case of forest and trees.

*The **Barrack Obama** has a very clearly formulated agenda and game-plan that they persistently strive to deliver day in and day out:

> Formulating a game-plan after thoroughly investigating all angles;

> Scrupulously anticipating where quicksand awaits;

> Slowly and meticulously gathering supporters with like-minded beliefs but varying backgrounds, ages, ethnicities and skill sets;

> Encouraging criticism and feedback…even when it hurts;

> Not allowing time to become the enemy but rather the catalyst for encouragement; and,

> Holding fast to the the core values of who you are and what you were raised to do.

The best parts of my journey through university and my career have involved unrelenting persistence. Of all traits, it has been the cornerstone and hallmark of my personality and success.

4. Attitude can protect you in a "world in crisis"

The fallout from this global economic meltdown will be deep and long. No matter what you read, there is no quick fix. The problems that tore at the basic infrastructure of the global financial institutions were long in the coming and could have been avoided. Greed and envy are incredible motivators in blinding people to the results of their actions. Plutarch wrote, "Imbalance between rich and poor is the oldest and most fatal ailment of all Republics." And if you look over the past 2000 years of dynasties decaying and losing power, there is one common ingredient: too much power and wealth controlled by few people. It's astounding how history continues to repeat itself and yet our governments don't seem to learn from the past.

How do you fit into all of this "global" mess? How do you maintain your sanity and not become overwhelmed with so many problems beyond your control?

First, shut yourself off from excessive media exposure. Stop reading or watching the news for a week. Focus on those things that matter most to you in your life. Do you know what those are? Through my first two books, you will have followed my thoughts about understanding who you are, and how to become the best person you can be. I shared with you lessons on improving your time efficiency and bolstering your attitude to tackle life like a wonderful adventure. This is the perfect time to put these lessons into practice.

The world is in crisis mode and the monstrous government debt that has been accumulated to keep our capitalistic game afloat is staggering. My counsel in shutting off the news is to not metaphorically-speaking, bury your head in the sand. It is merely to help you not become overwhelmed by the tumultuous media frenzy being fed by every inkling of bad news about unemployment or drops in the GDP. Unimaginably so, these trying times call for balance, digging in and forging ahead with cautious optimism. **There will be opportunities that cross your pathway. If you have the presence of mind, you will be able to grab them before others have had a chance to see what you've figured out.**

Secondly, keep very close to your family and talk with your significant other, your children and your friends about what is going on. Discussion is a great unifier and stress reducer if you keep the issues in perspective and don't try to solve what you can't. Determine those things in life that you can influence and focus on influencing them. Determine what in life that you cannot possibly influence and stop worrying about it. As I'm sure a few of you will learn in the years to come, this is one of the first lessons taught to new members at Alcoholics Anonymous.

Thirdly, get exercise and sleep. Lay off the booze or other stimulants for a while. Work to be the fittest you've ever been in life. Step outside into the fresh air and walk until your feet get blisters. When you are feeling overwhelmed you may have a tendency to come home, flick on the TV or boot up the computer and sit there like a vegetable for three hours. Don't do that. Once this day is done it is gone forever.

Next, take nothing for granted including your job. No country, industry or company is insulated from this economy tsunami. Keep your eyes open for opportunities but do not grab at them all. Remember that your company, fellow employees and your customers are all feeling the same pressures, regardless of seniority or geography. **If you have a job, then make yourself invaluable at work**. If you customarily bring forward one initiative a month…make it one stronger initiative every week. Ensure that senior people know who you are and see how you are stepping up to the plate.

While you are striving to keep your current job make solid efforts to set up a trap door: a job you could move to in the event that you are terminated. Do not be standing naively like a deer on the road about to be caught in the headlights. Watch the signs of how your company is really performing. This would be a good time to catch up with a Headhunter or two.

All of us will be under considerable pressures and strains over the next few years whether you already are in the work force or are sitting in a classroom trying to figure out what career you should be pursuing. Patience will be a much needed virtue. An attitude of respect will certainly help. A dose of understanding the jungle laws of survival of the fittest will come into play.

Finding the right balance within your attitude is what will separate the winners from the losers.

Chapter 6 Highlight:

Your generation is breaking into a workforce biased against your (supposed) sense of entitlement. Your parents and earlier teachers were well-meaning in breeding this high level of expectation into your wiring but it's going to hurt you if you don't recognize its shortcomings.

Your digital generation has a wealth of experience that the world needs. Don't sell yourselves short. Relook your attitude and decide what role persistence can play in helping you achieve your goals. As political and financial upheavals continue to barrage our sanity, be brave and on the lookout for both dangers and opportunities.

Chapter 7

Balance the four cornerstones of your health

"Housekeeping ain't no joke..."

-Louisa May Alcott

I've challenged you to rethink your attitude, your persistence and how to be brave in the face of uncertainty. I've been almost derisively clear about how other generations are viewing you. I realize this is a lot to take in. So let me shift gears and use this chapter to talk about bringing a proper equilibrium into the four cornerstones of your health. This balance is a lot like housekeeping. It's something you have to keep at day after day. Finding this balance in your life can't start at a better place than when you are at school and just embarking on your career.

The four cornerstones I want to discuss in this chapter are:

A. The physical game

B. Emotional/psychological harmony

C. Your mental well-being

D. The spiritual side of you

Why the concern with balance?

Most people reluctantly think about "life balance" when: a) they turn forty; b) someone close to them dies or becomes stricken; or, c) they themselves become ill. In my early 40s I started noticing that I was experiencing new aches and loathsome pains from normal exercise that pre-40 didn't make me break a sweat. I found that my recovery from hard physical workouts was much longer. My sleep patterns shifted and I started awakening at the oddest hours to go to the bathroom. How did my bladder know that I had turned 40? Why did my health begin to change so suddenly? Where was that youthful invulnerability that I thought would protect me from harm…and aging?

Most of you reading this are in your late teens and early 20s with our youthful belief of invulnerability. You are fit as can be: can drink like a fish; eat like a horse; party like there's no tomorrow; and, sleep like a log. So humor me for a chapter as I share some thoughts about health and balance.

Over the past five years, a lot of people I personally know announced they were battling cancer, heart issues or some other frightening disease. I kept count on my fingers. Soon, I ran out of fingers and the unambiguous reality set in. People my own age were dying around me. I was dismayed and frankly couldn't understand how all these young people my own age could be inconceivably dying and being annihilated? You see, even at 50+, I still consider myself young. Most days I think of myself being like you.

After ponderous consideration, here is what I came to understand.

We all have due dates stamped on us when we are born. Give or take, those due dates can be brought forward or delayed by how we conduct ourselves and live our lives. Contrary to what most of you believe (and what I believed at your age) none of us is invulnerable. Regardless what we do, there are diseases out there quite capable of infiltrating and systematically obliterating our immune systems. The mystery is whether one of those diseases has your name on it.

Don't misunderstand me. I'm the farthest from being a fatalist. That's not how I intend to play this game.

But from what I've observed, certain ailments and diseases are going to come your way no matter what you do. I know people dying of lung cancer who don't smoke: People with ominous heart issues who exercise like Olympians.

So here is what I have determined and set out to do. I want to nimbly cheat death or at least delay my "due date" as long as is humanly possible. I want to be around in a healthy mental and physical state for my children and their children. There's a lot I want to do and frankly, one life just isn't enough time. So my thinking is pretty straight-forward even if it may sound naïve.

I'm going to do everything physically, mentally, emotionally and psychologically possible to prepare myself in the event that some bastard disease or contemptible ailment is inadvertently scheduled to come my way. I don't intend to be a good soldier and "fade away into that gentle night." I'm going to fight like a banshee every step of the way.

I have a profound inclination that the sooner you appreciate this viewpoint and begin to act upon it, the longer, and healthier you are going to live. And by the word "sooner," I mean today.

A. The physical game

I'm going to retard the erosion of age and gravity on my person. I'm not going to drink alcohol, ingest drugs, smoke cigarettes, over-eat cholesterol or fatty foods. I'm going to adhere to a fitness regime that pushes me to the limit and balances my cardiovascular, muscular and overall physical well-being. I'm going to get lots of sleep and fresh air. I'm going to have yearly medical physicals and will listen to my doctor. I am prepared to endure any unpleasant medical procedures if they will help identify an issue early in the game. I want to know at all times with what I'm dealing that might affect my due date.

Rob Bruce is the President of Rogers Wireless in Canada. He is the epitome of a highly successful businessman who recognizes the importance of physical fitness, balance and well-being. He exercises like a fiend and meticulously watches his diet. Like me, he intends to be the best he can be and is prepared to do what it takes. His exercise regiment is time consuming and if a senior person with his workload and responsibilities can make it work, then so can you.

Recently Rob sent me a fabulous book entitled, "Younger Next Year." Authors Chris Crowley and Dr. Henry S. Lodge talk about turning back your biological clock. In this book, Crowley and Lodge share how men can avoid 70 percent of the decay and eliminate 50 percent of the injuries and illnesses (associated) with getting older. I love the simplicity and logic of their 7 lessons:

1. Exercise six days a week for the rest of your life.
2. Do serious aerobic exercise four days a week for the rest of your life.
3. Do serious strength training, with weights, two days a week for the rest of your life.
4. Spend less than you make.
5. Quit eating crap.
6. Care.
7. Connect and commit.

Frankly, none of their 7 themes is rocket science. It's just plain old-fashioned common sense. The thread to their book is doing something "for the rest of your life." You will be no good to anyone if you lose your health and physical well-being.

B. <u>Emotional/psychological harmony</u>

This cornerstone of your health is much more difficult to work on. When you are not emotionally stable, the world can be a pretty rough and persecuting place. Every day can seem apocalyptic. The current pressures we are all facing are certainly not going to help students entering a pressured job market. Emotional unrest can be the root of many of evils from sleep deprivation, to eating disorders, to drug dependencies or to career problems. How much of your emotional stability is around the relationships you have with your families and friends? The cause of emotional unrest may go further back than you know.

I'm no shrink but I've observed enough to be able to share a few thoughts.

The first step is to recognize that you need help, or that someone close to you needs help. Turning away from this realization won't heal it. Open wounds have a way of festering and never healing.

The second step is to realize that it is okay that you need help. Life isn't a game meant to be played alone. At various times in everyone's life we need to reach out to someone else. **Why are all of our egos so**

frail that we fear displaying the vulnerability to ask for help? It's okay to put up your hand and say, "I'm in trouble. I need help." Not all problems can be solved personally or through your family and friends. It's okay to need someone else. Please repeat this last sentence. "It's okay to need someone else."

The third step is to reach out to someone with the expertise to help you. This may be professional counseling. There are many charlatans professing expertise because they took a few courses. Don't fall prey to them. Seek certified professional help. Your medical doctor can help with referrals. Some people feel more comfortable talking to their Priest, Minister or Rabbi. Just ensure that the qualifications are in order.

Fourth, allow the proper time for you to get back on track. Don't set preconceived timelines. Neither you nor your parents are the experts so don't create an artificial timeline. All that will do is intensify the pressure you are already experiencing.

And finally, be honest with yourself when you are with that expert. Don't try to mask the situation. Your hand is out there for help. Let the experts do their job. Be patient with yourself and know that everything will be okay. I realize that a lot of my contemporaries will remember a poem that gained great awareness in the 1960's called *The Desiderata*. It is one of the most touching messages I've ever read and it always helped to settle me down when I was your age. It's worth a Google when you are feeling overwhelmed and don't know which way to turn.

C. <u>Your mental health</u>

I had a strange thought when I was scanning the recent Statistics Canada's findings around the issue that Canadians are getting fatter. It seems that there's more pronounced obesity amongst our children and teenagers then five years ago. Wow, there's a blinding glimpse of the obvious. Rarely do I see kids playing outside on the street or in playgrounds. That's because like the adults surrounding them, they're inside their houses watching The Family Guy or South Park. They are on their computers or X-Boxes and PS3 players playing mindless games where something is being killed, destroyed or stolen. They are texting the kid next door rather than standing up, putting on a coat and walking across the driveway to say hello. They are living on Facebook rather than going to their friend's houses and having a face to face interaction.

What's for dinner? Well, McDonald' sales are through the roof over the past 5 years. Is this in reaction to rising food prices and grocery bills that have skyrocketed? Or is this in part because Canadians are addicted to fast food restaurants or our Canadian national past-time of Tim Horton's donuts and treats?

So why on earth should we be surprised by, or alarmed with the most recent numbers on obesity from Statistics Canada?

I wondered what the numbers from Statistics Canada would be for the shape our mental faculties. I don't recall seeing any numbers on this. Every so often there will be a report issued on the overall level of scholastic achievement by our students. Invariably it shows that our Canadian kids are falling behind in the core subjects versus their counterparts in other countries. However, wouldn't it be fascinating if a study was conducted that compared the mental acuity of our post 18 year-old Canadian adults versus contemporaries in other countries? I'd love to see the results of that study over the past ten years.

You see, there is a real debate on what's happened within your Net Gener group because of your technically-oriented upbringing. Here are the three key components as I see them in the form of tangible questions:

1) How have Net Geners' mental capabilities been affected by having spent so much time on their computers?

2) Has the whole game of multi-tasking helped or hindered kids as they move from High School to University to the working world?

3) Are Net Geners' socially inept because of their lack of face to face interpersonal activity?

There are contradictory findings to the answers to these questions. I marvel at your generations' ability to choreograph your way through the mounds of information on the Internet to find what you need. I'm blown away at your technical superiority with anything that plugs in and has a computer chip. Conversely, I am shocked by the amount of time that teenagers spend playing mindless and depraved computer games that are nothing more than "shoot'em up and kill'em real bad" videos that numb minds and destroy vision. Sure, it's a great way to help hand/eye contact and motor skills: so is playing outside with fresh air and other human beings.

As for the arguments around multi-tasking versus focusing on one or two actions at a time, there is just as much contradictory evidence. For my two cents worth, I need to focus on one thing at a time. Sure, I can be pulled out mid-stream but I can't listen to music, work on my computer, flip over to send an e-mail, text a pal and watch NFL football. I can do any 1-2 of those actions but beyond that something is going to suffer and that's just plain common sense. My brain can only focus and give its best attention if it's not overloaded with too many tasks at once. If you plug in too many electric cords into a power outlet you will blow a fuse. I think a lot of fuses are already beginning to blow when you look at the dropout rate at universities.

Point 3 scares me. How do you learn to interact with other human beings when you spend your life expressing yourself through a keyboard on Facebook? How do you learn to read a room or see the gentle nuances of "body language" when almost all of your interaction is conducted on a phone or some other hand-held device? I can't imagine the strain that a lot of you are going to have when you find yourself in an office eight hours a day having to talk to people with your voice and not through your fingers. I realize there's a great comfort in being able to respond to a text message in your own time: carefully selecting your words. That's not reality. When you are face to face with another human being, you are going to need to be able to read their face and their movements as well as understanding their words. I think we have a whole society losing the understanding of the non-verbal communication that takes place in our world.

And thus the profound need for "mental" balance as one of your four cornerstones. Your brain is a muscle like your bicep or your abs. You need to exercise that muscle every day in a variety of ways. Your post High School education will help but it's only a start. What are you doing to strengthen your brain to better arm yourself for the next phase in your life? Here are some suggestions. Pick any three:

a) Read beyond the headlines: form deeper insights. Read

something printed. Join a book reading club. Go to a library for fun.

b) Research what's important to you as thoroughly as you possibly can

c) Take up Bridge with real people…not on your computer

d) Do the NY Times Crossword Puzzle with your friends

e) Study a foreign culture or language

f) Take up a new musical instrument and learn it from scratch

g) Memorize something new every day

h) Join school clubs that encourage debating and discussion

i) Play Sudoku every day

j) Read books that were written over fifty years ago

k) Travel somewhere to experience something new

You'll notice that the above list encourages you to interface with other people. Part of exercising your brain is learning how to quickly interface and communicate with people. The more you put yourself out there, the stronger your mental facilities will be.

Here's a fun and somewhat outrageous game I play to exercise my mind. This will give you an insight as to how warped my brain is. I label this my "James Bond" game and to this point in my life I haven't shared it with too many people. Here's how the game is played. When I enter a room I memorize everything in it. I count the windows and doors and determine the fastest way out of that room. I try to calculate the square footage and height. I look around the room and find ten items that could be turned into weapons. I know this isn't your usual game of Monopoly or flipping beer caps. I've been doing this game for years and it provides me more entertainment than most things I do. When I approach a stairwell, I estimate the number of stairs. When I'm walking towards a destination, I guess the number of steps. I memorize license plates and make up words using the letters like I would in a game of Scrabble. Okay, so I'm warped.

I recognized a long time ago that your mental well-being depends on you using your mind and exercising it. When you graduate there is a great relief that you're done with school, text books and exams. Allow me to repudiate that belief. When you graduate, your real learning has just begun. I'm not insinuating that your job is going to be the source of this new learning. In many cases, it won't be. If you depend on your company to mentally stimulate you then you will be sorely disappointed.

When you graduate, continue to find ways to learn and study and drive the well-being of your mind. Like any muscle, without exercise, your brain will atrophy and so will your career.

D. Your spiritual beliefs

The final cornerstone of your health is spiritual well-being. Do you have faith in anything beyond the Internet, your cell phone and your I-Pod? Do you attend church, a mosque or a synagogue?

I was raised a Roman Catholic and attended a Catholic Separate School until I was thirteen. The teachers included Nuns and Priests who damaged my faith in God more than they could ever know. The often cruel harshness of their institutionalized delivery was only offset by the abject foolishness of their archaic teachings. Questions from students were discouraged: infusing extreme levels of guilt in everyday pleasures was the norm. Real burgeoning spirits were euthanized by century-old dictums. Entire generations of women were emotionally scarred as they were forced to believe that their sex was inferior and only for the purpose of procreation. I won't even go near the legal actions the Church has been forced to address because of the inappropriate behavior of their Priests and the corresponding actions by the Church. I'll leave that to Linden MacIntyre and his Giller Award winning book, "The Bishop's Man."

I lost faith because of that pitiable religious upbringing and turned away from the Church. But with the passage of time, I realized that your faith and spiritual well-being did not have to be tied to one denomination or physical building. I was encouraged by the faith of friends who were Anglican, Presbyterian, and Jewish. By my 30s, I realized that it wasn't where you practiced your faith. It certainly wasn't whether your faith was written in the Bible, the Torah or the Koran. It is the fact that you find something in your heart in which you want to believe. It is settling yourself to know what principles you hold dearly in life; how you perceive the world came into existence; what you believe happens after death; and most importantly, how you believe you should be acting towards other people.

Martin Luther King Jr. said that, "Faith is taking the first step, even when you don't see the whole staircase."

Investigating your inner peace is crucial for your spiritual health…even if you don't come up with all the answers. At the least, try to come up with good questions. Just don't ignore this cornerstone or you won't find an overall equilibrium that makes you feel complete.

Striving for the illusive key of balance

I understand that school-life is destructive to any kind of balance in your life: the workload is horrific, the pressures to meet people are intense and the drive to complete assignments and achieve incredible grades is monumental. For a lot of students, their physical and emotional health take a severe beating, especially in first year of university or college. Being away from family and friends is a double-edged sword. Much sought-after freedom can be as confining as no freedom at all. My daughter Rosalind is an 18 year-old freshman and describes the first year syndrome as "living in a fishbowl." What an appropriate metaphor.

It's during your time in university or college that you might as well begin to understand the importance of striving for time balance. **After you leave school, you are going to find that it's damned near impossible to find an appropriate balance between how much time you must dedicate to your job versus what you can protect for your personal life.**

In the earliest stages of my career, I failed miserably in trying to discover how to balance work to non-work. I was still feeling the aftermaths of university which made it difficult to transition into a full time job…without the customary July-August hiatus. The freedom that I had enjoyed in university disappeared. There was no sleeping in and cutting classes anymore. I wasn't surrounded with my pals 24/7. I couldn't stay up all night chasing girls. I couldn't catch up on sleep during the day.

New to the workforce meant earning good money. It was great having a regular paycheck arrive until I faced the shock that most of your paycheck was being eaten up in taxes, rent, and insurance. While the paycheck made it more interesting, the workload was overwhelming. I had difficulty balancing work and non-work times. Keeping them separate was almost impossible. The work ethic thrust upon us encompassed ridiculous hours at the office and that rudely infringed on what should have been my personal time. I had one boss put up a sign on his door that stated in bold red letters, "If you're not here Saturday don't bother showing up on Sunday."

In those early years of my career, I did a lousy job having a personal life. Sports fell to the wayside. Reading for pleasure became a thing of the past. Friendships waned and my personal life went down the toilet. The more senior people in the organization for whom I worked told me that this was the way of life if you wanted to get ahead. The new kids worked an astonishing 60+ hours each week just to get into the game. As the months passed, I looked closer at the sources of those comments. I saw middle-aged guys who were out of shape, on second or third marriages, wearing rumpled suits and frankly, looking like they weren't going anywhere in life.

The senior people I grew to admire were still heavily involved with sports; taking interesting vacations; spending good family time; and overall, appearing to have found that "illusive key of balance" in their lives. Their careers also were burgeoning. I began studying them and gleaning everything I could. Now even 30+ years later, those mentors I watched proved me right. It was possible to find the illusive key of balance.

The first stage of my pursuit was determining what "balance" meant to me: not to anyone else...but solely to me. Here is what I conceived (and you will quickly understand the tie-in to this chapter):

1. I must be physically fit. I immediately scheduled regular times for exercise, playing squash and lifting weights. I avoided escalators and always took the stairs. Every lunch I got outside and walked for thirty minutes. I decided to walk rather than drive and learned that getting to bed earlier allowed me to get up earlier to do something physically-oriented.

2. I determined that diet was going to play a critical role to my energy level. I decided to cut back on my alcohol consumption (eventually I cut it out all together). I didn't smoke so that was easy. I had been skipping breakfast to catch up on sleep so I set out to eat a proper breakfast every morning and began learning about cholesterol, starch and protein before it was popular to do so. A book you might want to look into is by Dr. Peter J. D'Adamo entitled, "Eat Right 4 Your Type." In his book, Dr. D'Adamo investigates the role that your DNA and blood type play in the interaction with what foods and food combinations you are ingesting. Dr. D'Adamo writes, "When you use the individualized characteristics of your blood type as a guidepost for eating and living, you will be healthier, you will naturally reach your ideal weight, and you will slow down the process of aging."

3. I pursued challenges beyond the job that would occupy my mind: require planning; create excitement; and, help me grow mentally and physically. This is a really important lesson for you to consider. **Don't expect to get complete fulfillment from your job. That's just not going to happen.**

4. I needed to be more efficient and to extricate anything and anybody who wasted my time. I needed to optimize every hour to be totally effective at work which would then free up time for my non-work endeavors. I guarded my work "to do" list like crazy and wouldn't be suckered into taking on new projects without an equal number being removed. If you take on too much work, you'll end up doing a hap-hazard job on all your projects. I practiced saying "no" to my supervisor and not feeling guilty or threatened when I did.

5. I needed to philosophically stop separating work and non-work thinking. I eventually learned that it was okay to think about leisure time and relationships while you were at work. Similarly, it was okay to be playing basketball and have your mind drift back to the office. Drifting between the two worlds is healthy. Trying to place a mental and emotional barrier between them is a recipe for disaster.

6. **I would surround myself with outstanding people at work and at home.** People who would enable me to get complete my tasks faster and who knew the importance of doing the job right the first time. Getting it right the first time became monumental for me. I wanted team-mates who strived for excellence and would not become unhinged when obstacles surfaced. Friends away from work who would bolster me with their optimism and confidence. People who would tell me things I needed to hear… even if it stung to hear what I didn't want to hear.

7. The best balance in life would be getting paid for a job I loved and coming home to a wonderful person I loved. I embarked upon my quest to find the right person for me.

As soon as I focused my attention on the need for balance, both sides of the equation exploded with growth and success. In an odd way, I don't think I could personally have found success in my career without my personal life being in order. Conversely, I don't think I could have found success in my personal life without my career success. It's the true Yin and Yang in the universe.

Keeping the home fires burning

In discussing balance I often get asked about the relationship side of the equation. People seem to understand the need for balance but just can't swing it. They admit to being poor time organizers or procrastinators. Many say their biggest issue is finding a long term relationship that is fulfilling. In the world of Net Geners it appears that short-term "hook-ups" are rampantly hampering longer-term relationships. Do you find that?

How do younger Net Geners, or frankly anyone, find each other and survive in this harried world where successful longer-term relationships seem so hard to come by? How do young men know how to conduct themselves when the music they listen to and the videos they memorize show such disrespect for members of the opposite sex? Don't musicians realize that calling a woman a "bitch" in a song just isn't cool? In my youth, we learned about the female anatomy by looking at pictures of naked women in Playboy. As teenagers, a number of my pals were surprised to learn that real life naked women don't have staples in their stomach. Now, internet porn is rampant and viewers can see anybody doing anything with anything. It's vile and vulgar and distorting expectations that your generation should be considering in relationships. **It must be very confusing to understand your own sexuality in today's world of mixing genders where sexual boundaries are so murky and scintillating.**

My wife Martha and I are now married over 20 years which I know to you makes us really old farts. Our relationship began when I first phoned her to ask her out on a date. This was before the words 'texting or emailing' were popular. Ten minutes into the conversation we got into a real testy argument and she almost hung up on me.

Over the years, the strength of our relationship has shown us:

1. It is okay to disagree: in fact it's a necessity. We are two very strong-willed personalities who are very opinionated. This is not about a Rihanna/Chris interaction: it's about finding the proper balance of maintaining willpowers and compromising.

2. Giving the other person the benefit of the doubt is mandatory.

3. It's alright to take a breather during an argument. Sometimes a change of venue or a little time apart can allow tempers to cool and clearer heads to prevail.

4. It's hard to be mad with your mate when you are holding hands.

5. We aren't afraid to argue in front of the kids. How else do they see it's okay to argue with your loved one and the other person isn't going to desert you because you disagree?

6. I've learned not to bring in other family members' opinions… despite the fact they almost always agree with me.

7. It's okay to apologize after an argument. It's okay to say, "I'm really sorry we had that fight. I still think you're wrong, but I'm sorry we had the disagreement."

8. Being in a relationship doesn't mean giving up your personal brand or doing the things that you enjoy. Couples are strongest when they remain two individual people…not clones.

Chapter 7 Highlight:

Finding balance is paramount if you want to be happy, successful and live a long healthy life. Your physical, emotional, psychological and spiritual cornerstones must be in harmony for you to be at peace. If you take any of these cornerstones for granted you will die before your "best before" due date. Finding balance means accepting that your work and non-work lives must blend in unison without one unfairly overwhelming the other.

Chapter 8

Know what to spend and what to save

"The future belongs to those who prepare for it..."

-Ralph Waldo Emerson

Writing this chapter in the fall of 2009 is quite different than if I had been writing it 12-18 months ago. Back then, we were just getting introduced to sub-prime mortgages, Fannie Mae, Freddie Mac and AIG. Stories appeared daily about questionable lending practices by the largest of American financial institutions and CEOs parachuting into the sunset with obscene severance packages. All hell broke loose as Lehman Brothers closed shop and Citibank's worth plummeted like a thousand tons of steel succumbing to gravity on the top of their investors' heads.

We witnessed horrific staff cuts, the sinking of the American dollar and the disappearing act of consumer confidence. We heard from people whose equity had been given a mortal blow with losses of 25-50%; houses losing half of their value and exceeding the value of the mortgage; and, GM and Chrysler filing for Chapter 11 protection in the USA. Most frighteningly, we observed governments infusing cash into the financial systems and buying ownership in companies that created deficits that my grandchildren will be paying off. We were introduced to Bernie Madoff and all the people he meticulously duped out of fortunes despite earlier warnings about him having been given to the SEC. And then to cap off 2009, the world's most famous golfer transfixed our lurid imaginations with a scintillating sex scandal that proved that no one has any dibs on privacy. Wow, what a perilous 18th month rollercoaster ride from hell.

Imagine for a moment that you are forty years older than you are today. You and your wife have done all the right things. You started saving early and put a little away with each paycheck. Like your neighbors and co-workers, you trusted the company pension plans and invested every year. The family spending outlays were thoughtful with no unwarranted expenditures. You proudly paid off your mortgage costs as quickly as possible. Funds were held back for the kids to go to college and a little nest egg was put aside for a rainy day. Expectations were strong for government and company pension cheques in the next couple of years. Overall, a very sound family approach to fiscal planning.

And then 2008 came along and dashed everything you knew to be true. You and your wife are now facing the strain of a lifetime as your company pension plans are being demolished; well-earned RRSPs or 401Ks have been eviscerated; and, the house you were counting on to sell to help pay for your retirement has withered in value. Your healthcare and insurance costs are rising and there is a possibility that your company pension plan might disappear in the future if the company's performance doesn't turn around.

This is not a far-fetch fictional story. This is exactly what has happened to a lot of people across North America and beyond in the last twenty-four months.

It might sound somewhat callous but I've come to know that just when you think you've got it all going the right way, life happens. I know it's not very reassuring to those struggling to make ends meet. **It's just the unsympathetic reality that things in life have a way of going sideways when you least expect it**. That's why I want to dedicate a chapter to your finances just as you are launching your career. It's crucial you not fritter away one cent of your earnings without intending to.

Here is some practical counsel for thinking about your spending, investing and saving plans:

1. Get the best financial advice you can afford. This should not

include anyone trying to sell you anything, a relative or an insurance agent. Cross-check that advice with other experts.

2. Begin your planning by understanding what is important to you in life. What do you love doing? What are you spending today that you could see spending every day for the rest of your life? What possessions could you do without in the future? Can you see yourself being a parent in the future? Where might you want to live?

   There are a lot of questions to be answered before you can sit down and tackle an Excel spreadsheet or a financial planning guide. I realize that it is tremendously difficult to know what's coming at you in the future when you are still in your early 20s. That's why it's important to keep your financial planning philosophies flexible.

3. You have to start your planning process with a thorough and extremely detailed understanding of your outflows/spending before you can understand your longer-term savings plan. It's not rocket science to sit down and recount every dollar you've spent in each of the last 3 months. Are those 3 months representative of how your outflow's trend? Have you been fiscally responsible with your money or just letting it flow out in a stream of conspicuous consumption? My rule of thumb is simple despite the current ease at getting low rate mortgages or loans: **Don't spend what you haven't got.**

4. Here's a warning I was given that I foolishly ignored because of course, I thought I knew everything. Every time you get a raise in pay: your debts will grow, you'll have more credit cards, you'll take more trips, and, you'll have more clothes in your closet than you need. In short order, even at the higher salary level, you'll start to complain that your money just seems to disappear. Most people fall into that trap. Here's the advice I ignored:

   Try maintaining the same spending level even when your salary is increased.

In Thomas Stanley and William Danko's book "*The Millionaire Next Door,*" the authors write that, "Being frugal is the cornerstone of wealth-building."

It goes without saying that spending, and your inclination to spend will increase with pay raises, marriage, the arrival of children, changes in living accommodations and time. Please be cautious in not spending money simply because you can.

5. Once you've got a pretty steady handle on your spending you have to now understand "hidden costs" which will change with time. These costs will affect your inflow/earnings while dampening your ability to spend and save. Be en garde for: a) changes in income tax and special charges. Watch out for the modifications that appear with every new political administration; b) changes in interest rates for savings accounts; c) changes in interest rates for your credit card companies; d) increases in health/house/auto insurance premiums; e) hidden bank charges; f) cost of living price increases on your Telco/TV bills; g) increases in property taxes or purchasing/selling property taxes; h) increased deductions on your paycheck because of changes in company policies or benefit plans; and, i) hidden costs on travel/hotel/entertainment/car rentals. You may not be able to avoid these extra hurts, but at the least be aware so you can incorporate them into your planning.

6. Once you have your outflows on paper, compare them to Point 2. Are you missing out on anything you highly value in life? Are you spending in areas that you don't even consider important? Allocate your money where it is needed and wanted.

7. Understanding your inflows is vital. This is more than a quick perusal of your paycheck. **Make sure that your paycheck is correct**. In my last job, I discovered three months after the fact that I was being under-paid by my company. It was completely innocent and a simple accounting error but If I hadn't caught the mistake I might have been out of luck. Don't assume anything when it comes to your money.

Here are some other considerations for you to think about:

1. Do not deal with one financial institution. The lessons of 2008-09 were as clear a lesson you'll ever get.

2. Do not invest in get rich quick schemes. The faster you might earn extra money is nothing compared to the speed with which you might lose it.

3. Set up an automatic withdrawal from every paycheck when it is deposited. Do not let it sit in a low interest, daily account. Get it into a richer interest savings plan and leave it there.

4. Plan your overall portfolio to be 70% into longer-term, low risk and steady interest accrual. I know this is boring as boring can be. The number of times I told this to my pals and got shot down for investing like an old maid. Those are the same pals that invested 70+% into the higher risk/return equity world. Boy, were they badly financially spanked over the past two years.

5. **Surround yourself with people who do not waste money**. In "*The Millionaire Next Door*," authors Danko and Stanley write, "most people will never become wealthy in one generation if they are married to people who are wasteful. A couple cannot accumulate wealth if one of its members is a hyper-consumer."

6. Do not over-invest in insurance or real-estate. Look at the North American trends and it is not hard to see that housing slumps can swoop in without much hoopla. Understand all the costs involved with planning and buying if you intend to get into the "buy/upgrade/sell" game.

7. Become a global investor. Seeking opportunities outside North America is simply common sense. There are developing nations with huge investment opportunities waiting to be snatched up by the people with foresight and a few bucks. Take care to understand the full impact of currency exchanges.

8. Never head out to buy something that you really need and have

to have. To protect your money, you must always be prepared to put off any purchase and walk away from the bargaining table.

9. Business plans on spending and saving will change with your marital status. Your significant other may have different priorities to your own. You might want to discuss all of this before one of you moves in with the other.

Setting up a budget is not difficult if you review it regularly. There are numerous Excel budgeting programs and almost every bank site has a budget format you can download. Your overall budgeting should present a twelve month summary based on the calendar year. That will allow you to fully understand various cost cycles that hit in each of the months. Some monthly outlays will be lower than others. Certain costs will be fixed monthly like rent whereas other costs may be paid only in certain months of the year like insurance. Once you have set up a 12 month overview of your spending, you then allocate it monthly. Make sure you keep all receipts and copies of any expenditure to ensure you are on track to your budget.

Chapter 8 Highlight:

Start your career with a personal business plan of what to spend and what to save. The sooner you do this, the more financial stability you will create which in time will translate to mean peace of mind. Update your overall business plan every two years and spend against things that are important for your happiness. Do not depend on the government, your company, or anyone else to look after you financially.

Chapter 9

Superior communication abilities will drive your success

"If you have an important point to make, don't be subtle or clever. Use a pile driver. Hit the point once. Then come back and hit it again. Then hit it a third time...with a tremendous whack..."

-Sir Winston Churchill

When you start your career, people will form an opinion of you very quickly. It's not easy to turnaround that opinion once it's been made. Approach every interaction with the objective of taking the high ground and creating the best possible picture of your personal brand. Your verbal and written communication skills will set the tone of how this picture will look.

A. Verbally interacting with others

Your first interaction with a new person is all important. I ensure that I give my total attention, make direct eye contact, smile genuinely and offer a polite, yet firm handshake. Speak clearly and don't mumble. That first impression will hopefully last until we can make a more enduring connection with our words and thoughts.

If I've done my homework and know a few things about the person I'm meeting, I will offer up a question to try to ease the situation or any awkwardness that sometimes accompanies the simple word "Hello."

> "I understand you used to work for John Henderson. He speaks volumes on you. How long have you known John?"

> "Donald Wang was telling me that you've taken to running marathons. How are the knees holding up?"

Very simple questions can remove tension and show interest in wanting to engage in a conversation. I attempt to use the other person's name two or three times during our first interaction. I also consider what actor/actress the person most reminds me of: anything to form a memory. These tactics help me to remember their name later. Entering the working world, you are going to be meeting a lot of new people. After you meet someone, write down their name and what you talked about. I use file cards and they've always proved invaluable to me. Check the company phone list to ensure you have the right name and spelling.

The art of conversation seems to be waning

I was raised in a family where conversation and card-playing was paramount. Within minutes of guests arriving at our house, a deck of cards would appear, chairs would be rearranged and refreshments served. As the game progressed, the volume of conversation would increase with gales of laughter. Through the entire game, my parents and their guests would be carrying on 2-3 different highly animated conversations. As a kid, I would sit in wonderment that these adults felt so comfortable to voice, and share opinions. They would talk for hours about topics from world events to movies to the price of a pound of butter. When the game wrapped up, the conversation would continue.

Because of my upbringing in that small town playing field, I learned the value of being able to carry on a decent conversation. It helped me with fellow employees, business colleagues, people I was trying to date and in interviews for jobs. **Being able to genuinely engage someone in a profound conversation has gotten me out of potentially dangerous physical altercations and career limiting situations.** Conversing isn't all that hard. You need to have something to talk about and be willing to tactfully know how to involve another person. The former Prime Minister of England, Tony Blair said, "To carry on a decent conversation I've learned it's more important to be interested, than interesting."

Here are a few considerations in how you are verbally interacting with other people:

1. I tend towards a modicum of formality when I first meet someone. I guard against employing humor which might be offensive or off-putting.

2. Give the person with whom you are speaking your full attention. Don't look around for other familiar faces. I will state for the record that I don't think it's proper to accept phone calls, text messages or e-mails from a 3rd party during a conversation. If I am awaiting an emergency call, I will briefly explain that I might have to excuse myself for a minute of two. I will apologize profusely and make sure it's a one-time event. If you are talking with someone then have the decency to give them your attention.

3. **Never engage in political, religious or financial discussions with people unless you've known them for a long, long time.** I am prepared to listen, ask questions and learn. I've watched more friendships bite the dust because of philosophical differences on these 3 topics.

4. Be well-read on world events. Don't just know the hottest postings and headlines on YouTube or CNN. Read the guts of the news story and form your own opinions. Have something of interest that can make anyone's interaction with you engaging and involving. People enjoy talking about what they are reading.

5. Try to find out something interesting about the person with whom you are speaking. That's the joy of Google. People enjoy talking about something they know. Use questions to help unlock someone's confidence. Don't talk too much about yourself.

6. Don't name drop even if Paul McCartney is your first cousin.

7. The only opinions you should state about anyone else should be positive. If you have nothing good to say, say nothing.

8. Keep your hands to yourself. Do not move into the other person's space/comfort zone.

9. Do not discuss health or health issues unless it is around a very well-known and publicized issue like H1N1.

10. Understand that a conversation goes beyond the words being said. Look for physical clues that accompany the words. Body movements and facial nuances can tell you more about what the person is truly feeling than will their words.

B. How you use your computer to communicate

I'm not sure where to begin. As a CEO I get mountains of e-mails from clients, employees, spam, would-be suppliers, people looking for jobs, people seeking advice and family/friends. My computer's in-box refills the moment I empty it. Even the arrival of my Blackberry has only served to put a dent into the unceasing barrage of "stuff" coming my way. **It's hard to remember a time when I wasn't computer-bound and pathetically enslaved to the electronic world.**

When computers first arrived on my desk in the early 90's I started measuring my own immeasurable importance by how many e-mails arrived during the day: the more the better. Now twenty years later, I am overwhelmed and can only marvel that the vast majority of e-mails sent to me are unnecessary, poorly crafted, ill-thought out and useless.

Let me share some observations about e-mails that might help you as you enter the workforce. I say e-mails rather than text messages.

> Don't send an e-mail unless it's vital. Keep to core information the reader needs to know. Avoid red herrings in your communication. Less is more.

> Send an e-mail to avoid the potential for miscommunication.

> Don't copy someone just to show them what you've done.

> Just because you sent an e-mail doesn't guarantee your message had been received, acknowledged or agreed-to.

> Get to your point el pronto. State precisely what you want and what you need from the recipient.

> God created “spell check” for a reason. Use it religiously.

> Don’t use short forms or acronyms.

> Don’t be familiar with me if we haven’t met face to face.

> Don’t trust the receiver to keep your e-mail confidential or secure. It can be forwarded to people who might use it against you.

> Before pressing the “Send” button, ask yourself this question. “Would I be happy to see this e-mail splashed across the front page of the Wall Street Journal?”

> Never respond to a grenade e-mail. A grenade is one of those highly unprofessional e-mails people send to show their anger, dissatisfaction or disgust with another person. They tend to be obnoxious and rude. It’s cyber-bullying in an office setting. You’ll know when you receive a grenade because your heart will pound uncontrollably and your tendency will be to respond immediately. Don’t do that even you have irrefutable evidence that the sender is 100% incorrect and lying through their little bastard teeth. Nothing is ever gained by lobbing back a written grenade. Leave your office and get some air: calm down. Realize you are dealing with a grenade. Take great care to understand what has been sent to you and ensure that the facts, as stated in the grenade, are not correct. With facts in hand, go to your supervisor with a copy of the grenade e-mail. Tell him/her that you intend to confront the person in a very professional manner copying your own boss and the sender’s boss. In your response, you acknowledge the e-mail you received and simply clarify some misunderstandings. Offer a face to face meeting if your explanations aren’t clear or satisfactory. Suggest that when future issues arise perhaps the sender would pick up the phone or arrange a meeting so that his/her misunderstanding can be rectified. Finally, your last sentence will be to thank the person for sending you the note. Take the high ground.

C. Communicating in a business setting

I encourage university and college professors to focus on students' presentation skills. Some of us are born to stand up before an audience and talk. We get the initial butterflies but then settle down and deliver our message. For the majority of people this is a frightening experience. Regardless of your profession, there will come a time when you need to make presentations. Your audience will have great difficulty relating to, and accepting your message if you appear unduly nervous, anxious or downright terrified. You must make your audience feel comfortable with you so that they want to hear every word you have to say. There are hundreds of books on how to deliver a proper speech. Get one and take it to heart. Accept every invitation to speak in front of your fellow students and professors. Have yourself video-taped so that you and others can analyze and critique your performance. My most poignant rule for people giving speeches is very simple: know your topic inside out and don't forget to breathe.

D. Arming your skills by speaking more than one language

Richard Branson is one of those world-altering personalities that you can't help but admire. He is quoted as saying, "*Business opportunities are like buses. There's always another one coming along.*" The difference today is that the next bus contains parts made in China and Russia. The glass for the windshield was possibly made in Brazil. The driver was born in Mumbai. So when that bus comes along in the future, how will you know that your fellow passengers speak English as a first language? Those passengers could be potential employers, competitors or personal significant others.

Come to the realization that in this century, the English language will loosen its strangle-hold on the rest of the planet. I believe that Mandarin will grow monumentally in linguistic importance by 2100. Why should 1.33 billion Chinese; 1.15 billion Indians, and 960 million Brazilians have to kowtow to English? In the near future, North American companies won't be sending ex-pats to run their operations outside the USA. These offices will be run by locals who speak the language (and likely English), have local contacts, know the local customs and have been raised to succeed in their own back yard: after having possibly studied in the USA, Canada or England.

In the future, the current developed nations will be competing against far superior, locally-owned and operated companies with stronger ties to their consumer base. These competitors will have an eye to looking at expanding internationally into our own back yard…if in fact, they even need to look in our back yard for customers given their incredibly large consumer bases. (In the future, will a skyrocketing price of oil dampen the taste for Eastern companies to want to transport and sell their products to the USA? Jeff Rubin dealt with this issue of rising oil prices in a fabulous book called, "Why Your World Is About to Get a Whole Lot Smaller.")

If you speak only English, you will be limiting yourself in the years to come. It's like only being able to shoot or dribble a basketball with your right hand. Not too hard for your competition to take the ball away. Especially when you consider that the ball you are dribbling and the sneakers you are wearing were both made in a Chinese plant. By the way, so was the referee's whistle and the net at which you are shooting.

Chapter 9 Highlight:

Don't go to a lot of effort creating a wonderful personal brand unless you communicate that brand optimally and professionally under any circumstances. Learning a second language can open up a world of business opportunities while exercising your mind and opening up doors to different sides of your personality.

Chapter 10

Nurture and protect your integrity

"You will soon break the bow, if you keep it stretched..."

-Phaedrus

According to the Webster dictionary, integrity is "an adherence to a code of values." But what is today's "code of values" against which you are supposed to adhere?

Like most Net Geners, my children are totally confused about "today's code of values." In the last five to ten years Rosalind and Christian have grown up witnessing the deterioration of societal cornerstones and values. They've experienced: the horror of 9/11 while living in Chicago; the ongoing deterioration of the Church around sexual abuse allegations; the economic tsunami that has pummeled global financial stability; the rise of terrorism and suicide bombers; and, political maelstroms across the globe. Whether I like it or not, they are exposed to music videos visually presenting a bashing of women. It seems that movies have taken gore and violence to an obscene level of degradation while the internet has made supplying and buying porn a multi-billion dollar business. YouTube brings sensationalistic uncensored videos that show the underbelly of our society and humanity. How horrible would it be if an alien civilization was to judge humanity on the visual and audible trash we are exposing to our children.

Given all of this flying at us every day, how is anyone supposed

to know what "code of values" their integrity is supposed to be built upon?

I can be such a simpleton at times: old fashioned and boring as dishwater. But I'm a simpleton with a very clear cut view of what is right and what is wrong. I won't go into that broad-shouldered rant in this book. You can read my sobering perspective in my first book. Rather, in this chapter I'll focus on the interplay of your working environment and your belief systems pertaining to personal integrity. Here are valid examples of what you are going to encounter when you hit your first job. Don't be fooled by the obviousness of the answers. Knowing the right answer and actually doing the right thing is not always as easy as you might hopefully believe.

1. In many industries you will need to record your time on an hourly basis. You must do this honestly and never pad your hours to make it look like you put in more effort than you did. These hours often determine how your company generates revenue which has tax implications with the government. Falsifying your time is cheating. If you are directed by a supervisor to "doctor" your timesheets and document hours that are not correct you must not comply. Go to a more senior person or to the Human Resources Department. Simply because a supervisor tells you to do something doesn't make it the right thing to do. Employ your own judgment.

2. Expense reports are designed to repay expenditures made by employees on the company's behalf. It will be very tempting to submit an extra cab receipt or a restaurant bill to make a few extra bucks. **Even if your boss directs you to add something to an expense report you must decline if it is not truthful**. Falsifying expense reports is stealing no matter how you look at it. It is automatic grounds for dismissal and the moniker of being a thief will stick with you forever.

3. It will be tempting to take office supplies home. Employee theft is a major issue in most companies. Could you imagine being caught and fired for taking ten or twenty dollars worth of office supplies? That misjudgment could derail your career. Don't take what isn't yours no matter who else is doing it in

the company. (On a sub-note, I guarantee a good number of you reading this have illegally pirated music. Don't kid yourself that pirating isn't theft).

4. When you are absent from your job then someone else has to take on your duties. For you to fake illness and increase someone else's workload isn't just unfair, it's downright rude. Only call in sick when you are sick.

5. **Treat all other employees with respect even if they will never be in a position to help your career: especially if they will never be in a position to help your career.** I can always judge the true fabric of a person by how they interact with the most junior people in the company.

6. Do not misuse company time by excessively checking Facebook, texting or e-mailing friends. Be reasonable.

7. If you have nothing positive to say about your company then don't say anything at all in a public forum. You never know who is within hearing distance and how that could backlash to damage your company...and/or you. I was in a restaurant a couple of years ago and couldn't help but eavesdrop on the adjoining table. Two employees of a competitive agency were discussing how much trouble their company was facing on a certain client. The two had no idea who I was or how loudly they were speaking. By 4:00pm that same day I had spoken to the CEO of the client in question and arranged for a pitch by my company. We got the business.

8. During WWII there were posters all over England that read, "Loose lips sink ships." The same applies to your company. You will find yourself in possession of confidential information. The word "confidential" means keeping your mouth shut: don't discuss this with family or friends. Frankly the same thing applies to your own personal business and privacy which I've mentioned in my discussion about what you are giving away on Facebook and Twitter.

9. Early in your career you will be faced with some sort of a bribe

from a supplier or non-company business associate. It could be as simple as: free tickets; an invitation to dinner; a bottle of Scotch; an I-Pod at Christmas; or clothes. **In my career, I've been offered trips, clothing, golf paraphernalia, money, sporting tickets, dinners, watches and booze. Hell, I've even been offered sex.** Don't ever take anything unless you expect to do something for it in return. Don't be bought.

10. Always make any interface with your company's customers honest and true. Never misrepresent the quality or value of your product or services. Don't try to pull a fast one on your customers by charging them more than is fair. Represent your company and product with the utmost of pride and sincerity. The public will reward you for this. Maltreat someone or misrepresent your company and be prepared for an onslaught of negativity in the world of social media. Never jeopardize your company's name, or your own.

Chapter 10 Highlight:

Your integrity is the richest element of your soul. Don't be tempted by offers of money, title or promotions to ever gamble with your integrity. All of those things are fleeting. Your name isn't.

Always remember that every action has a reaction and even little transgressions can incite monumental backlashes. Breaching your integrity and bending the rules inappropriately will encourage others to believe it is okay for them to do likewise.

Pre-epilogue:

If I knew at your age what I know today. . .

I wish someone had done this for me when I was still in school or just embarking upon my career.

Part of me envies your youth and the fact that you are just starting out on a very exciting journey. And then I consider the innumerable strains you must be feeling as you try to discover your way through such a convoluted and wounded job market. In this world of computer-driven socialization I wonder how you will approach face to face, human interactive relationships: Is your generation the manifestation of Ayn Rand's novella, "Anthem?"

I've taken the liberty of sharing the top ten lessons I wish I had known when I was your age. Perhaps a point or two may help you recalibrate to help your chances at success.

1. **Invest yourself for all you are worth in your school.** I floated through university and didn't do anything beyond what was expected of me. It's fair to say that I simply "showed up." I regret that. Look beyond your curriculum. What clubs can you join? Look into the sports facilities where you can learn a martial art or to scuba dive: both will be less expensive than when you graduate. Take advantage of what your school has to offer by investing yourself. The more you put into it…the more you will get out of it.

2. **Learn for the right reasons.** University and college are not just about grades, a diploma or degree. It's about arming

yourself for the future. Engage in courses that are going to bolster your skill set and make you more ruthlessly competitive in the marketplace. Learn because it is going to help you...not because you're prepping for an exam.

3. **Surround yourself with the most talented, positive, and motivating people you can find.** Seek these people early in your life and then nurture your relationships post school. I've lost track of too many outstanding people throughout my career. Along the way, you will encounter fools who try to latch onto you. Don't allow that to happen. Never suffer a fool.

4. Set audacious goals that are going to require you to stretch to your physical and emotional limits. **Do not set out to achieve achievable goals. Set out to achieve the unachievable.** Jeffery Archer wrote an inspiring novel entitled, "Paths of Glory." It's the true story of a world-class mountain climber in the 1920s. George Mallory tackled and climbed every worthwhile mountain on the planet...except Chomolunga, Goddess Mother of the Earth. After three attempts on Mount Everest in 1924, it killed him. The interesting fact is that Mallory determined himself to climb Everest when he was still a young teenager. What's your Everest?

5. Remove geographical blinders in understanding your playing field. Look beyond North America for opportunities and risk. Taking an international career route will upgrade your life tool box like you can't imagine.

6. **Never make a decision without understanding the difference between "believing" something to be a fact and "knowing" something to be a fact.** I've watched more people walk blindly into quicksand because they didn't know the difference between these two words. Until you "know" something, it is not a fact. Go to the source to determine what is factual before you decide on anything. Do I need to mention anything about the word "assume?"

7. "Having a duty and obligation to my community and country"

are more than mere words. In his book, "*Johnny Bunko,*" Daniel H. Pink writes that, "truly successful people deploy themselves in the service of something larger than themselves: they leave their companies, their communities and their families a little better than before."

8. Life is what you make it. It's up to you to grab hold of your dreams and aspirations and go for them for all you are worth. Don't be dismayed by others' negativity or small-mindedness. Focus on what you can affect, not things beyond your control. The *Serenity Prayer* was written in 1934 by American theologian and teacher Reinhold Niebuhr. It's one of the foundations of Alcoholics Anonymous. It reads, "God, give us grace to accept with serenity the things that cannot be changed, courage to change the things which should be changed, and the wisdom to distinguish the one from the other." The word "God" can be modified to your religion.

9. Don't marry young. Take your 20's to: get to know who you are; successfully establish your personal brand; and, create a healthy bank account. **Don't allow anyone to rush you into a relationship commitment before you are ready.** Prenuptial agreements are not a reflection that you don't love the other person. They are an indication that you have a brain and are looking out for each other.

10. **Take life seriously but don't take yourself too seriously.** You can do all the things that I've outlined in this book and still keep your mindset healthy, positive and optimistic. Keep "you" in perspective. Whenever I need to refresh myself on this point, I look into the night skies and consider that I'm just a momentary spec in the universal continuum. Life has an astonishing way of working itself out if you can manage to keep laughing and not drive yourself crazy along the way.

Epilogue

The memory of that oppressive toothpick factory is surreal. It's hard to imagine that there was a time when I stood half-asleep staring at a white-washed brick wall trying to keep my fingers attached to my hands. But now in my 50's, I've come to know that it was exactly during that time in my life that my future took root. The guideposts I determined that summer helped steer my way from chopping toothpicks to having a very lucrative career, and an unimaginably happy and fulfilling life.

As you think about tomorrow, allow me to offer one final caution. It is monumentally critical that you use time to your advantage. Do not allow the years to become your enemy. Start considering how you can be more successful as you embark upon your career. Prepare your tomorrow today.

I fervently believe that your generation possesses talent and soul that this planet desperately needs. I also know that you have it within your power to be the best person you can be no matter what the world throws at you.

I hope you enjoyed *The Toothpick Factory.*

E-mail me at howard.breen@hbideation.com

Howard J. Breen May 2010

Addendum One

Personal Branding Exercise

Step One

So let's begin this personal branding exercise by going back in time before you hit puberty and went through the jading onslaught of teenage years: which is enough to suck the life and cripple the optimism out of anyone.

Think back to when you were eleven years old. For some of you this will be a shorter exercise than others. You might even enlist the memories of your parents or siblings. Fill this out in pencil, not pen. I guarantee that if you redo it tomorrow, or in a week, your answers will be different. A very wise CEO client of mine asked me this brilliant question over dinner with our wives.

"Howard, what were you like when you were eleven years old?"

I translated this question into a thinking process that I've outlined to help you formulated a richer, more relevant answer.

A. Step One: When I was eleven years old:
I wanted to be

____

____

____

____

The positive things that influenced me the most were

When I think of school and my friends I remember

When I think of my home and my neighborhood, I feel

There were things that bothered me like

What I liked best about myself was

What really embarrassed me was

____

____

____

This can be one of the most powerful exercises you can do for your personal brand: if you do it honestly. You don't have to share this with anyone. Hell, you can rip it up and throw it out if you don't like what you remember. But here's the rub. Until you dig deeply into your eleven year-old psyche, you can't understand from whence you've come and that's vital to understand how you became the person you are today. So don't coward out in this exercise. Do it properly and honestly before we go on. Don't be shy about involving your parents or friends. They can remember things about you that you might have forgotten…or chose to bury deep in your memories.

The vast majority of people I would term happy and successful in their careers are doing something that reflects the way they saw life as pre-teen children.

Conversely, the unhappiest people I come across are those whose jobs and careers are completely disconnected to the hopes they dreamed and fostered when they were eleven.

<u>Step Two</u>

Once you have constructed a factual recollection of your history you can evolve your analysis to the current tense and Step Two.

The second stage in developing your personal branding is to understand the consistencies and inconsistencies between how you see yourself and: a) the way others see you; b) your actions in life; and, c) the way you are allocating your time. This exercise will depict the consistencies and inconsistencies in how your actions and behavior compliment or contradict your inner self. This is a real eye-opener in the goal of finding comfort in your own skin.

Let me put this into a practical example.

Caitlin Clark is an 18 year-old sophomore who has good grades, diligent study habits and a cheerful, honest personality. She is very dedicated to her family and friends. It's always been a goal of hers to get an MBA and then study Law. On paper, Caitlin is certainly capable of achieving her goals, but in reality she may not. The obstacle that might de-rail her dream is that her actions are totally inconsistent with how she wants to be perceived. Every weekend Caitlin parties hard and doesn't leave until she is staggering drunk. Friends have posted very revealing photographs of her "in flagrante delicto" on Facebook pages. Some photos are even posted on Caitlin's own page. Like most other younger users of the vehicle, Caitlin doesn't understand that these pictures are now permanently imbedded the internet and can be retrieved indiscriminately in the future. Several of Caitlin's supposed pals have forwarded photos of Caitlin to the Facebook pages of several of her professors.

You know a "Caitlin" in your life. "Caitlin" could be Sean, Peter, Ashwin, Wang or Natasha. Is Caitlin you? I wonder what kind of an endorsement Caitlin is going to get from her professors when she applies to Law School. I wonder what will happen to all those Facebook pages and photos in 8 years when Caitlin is applying for a job.

Intently scrutinize every photo and word that represents you on your Facebook pages. Is there anything that you wouldn't want your parents or a future employer seeing? Be aware of cameras in the room when you might not be representing yourself in an optimal light. Don't allow recordings of today's indiscretions haunt your future. It's your privacy and your name. Protect it.

Your actions must at all times be consistent with how you see yourself and wish others to see you. You must surround yourself with people who reflect your personal brand values. Generating belief in your brand takes a lot of time and effort. Blowing the value of your personal brand takes a nanosecond. Just ask Tiger Woods about the goodwill and endorsements he's lost since the end of November.

B. Step Two: Today….

I would honestly describe myself as being

____

____

____

____

These are reasonable descriptors because

____

Most of my non-school, non-working time is spent

The top 3 words that I would use to describe myself would be

I behave and act consistently with how I see myself when I

My family would describe me as being

My friends and school pals (or co-workers) would describe me as being

My professors (or my boss) would describe me as being

____

____

____

____

Inconsistencies with how I act versus how I see me include

____

____

____

____

Inconsistencies with how others see me differently than I see myself might be

____

____

____

____

People with whom I surround myself that reflect my personal brand are

____

____

____

____

People who don't reflect my values and could be hurting my personal brand are

____

____

____

____

This section is very difficult. I hope it took more than ten minutes. If you want to complete it thoroughly, you need to engage others. Here's my rule of thumb: if your family or friends fill this out and there isn't one surprise for you then: a) you are being lied to by caring people who don't want to hurt your feelings; b) you've asked people who don't really know you well enough to fill this out; and/or, c) your actions/ persona are consistent with how you see yourself which might be good or bad depending on the feedback.

If you are already into the work force then you need to engage your co-workers and your supervisor. Get a written job description if you don't already have one. Don't begin a journey without a road map.

Step Three

The final step is to review and compare Steps One and Two. Are there similarities between how you looked at life when you were eleven and what you are doing today? My experience tells me that there should be something relevant between the two stages of your life. What learning can you bring forward to drive the consistency between the dreams of your youth and how you are conducting your life today?

Step Three is the map and the action plan. It is designed to have you take a hard look in the mirror and honestly decide if you like who is looking back at you. This stage is corrective action to get you in control of your future.

B. Step Three: Looking to the future

Things I admire about myself that I want to protect and nurture include

____

____

____

____

I had forgotten when I was eleven how much I enjoyed

____

____

____

I need to see more of these people who help me to be my best

I need to stop hanging around with these negative people who drag me down

Actions that promote me well include

I must stop these actions that are making my target audiences see me differently than I see myself

The three biggest emotional or intellectual changes I want to incorporate into 'how I see me' would include

Three physical changes I want to incorporate into 'how I see me' include

____

____

____

____

Three people who can help me transition to my stronger personal brand are

1. ________________________

2. ________________________

3. ________________________

I need to spend more of my time doing things like

____

____

____

____

Milestones (dates/events) against which I'll judge my performance include

____

____

____

____

This is the completion of the three stage personal branding exercise. Review it every 6-9 months to gauge your progression. It's up to you to make sure that how you conduct your actions and spend your time mirrors consistently with how you want to be seen by others. **Seriously consider how all decisions and choices you are making will help you succeed.**

Bibliography and Recommended Reading:

Archer, Jeffery. *Paths of Glory.* New York: St. Martin's Press. 2009

Armour, Stephanie. *Generation Y: They've Arrived at Work with a New Attitude.* USA Today, November 6, 2005.

Breen, Howard J. *A page from a CEO's Diary.* Bloomington, Indiana. AuthorHouse. 2009.

Cohan, William D. *House of Cards: A Tale of Hubris and Wretched Excess on Wall Street.* New York: Doubleday Publishing Group. 2009.

Crowley, Chris, and Henry S. Lodge. *Younger Next Year: A Guide to Living Like 50 Until You're 80 and Beyond.* New York: Workman Publishing. 2004.

D'Adamo, Peter J. *Eat Right For Your Blood Type: The Individualized Diet Solution to Staying Healthy, Living Longer & Achieving Your Ideal Weight.* New York: G.P. Putnam's Sons. 1996.

Lancaster, Lynne C., and David Stillman. *When Generations Collide: Who They Are, Why They Clash, How to Solve the Generational Puzzle at Work.* New York: Collins, 2003.

Marston, Cam. *"Motivating the 'What's in it for me' Workforce."* Hoboken, N.J., Wiley. 2007.

Menzies, Gavin. *1421: The Year China Discovered The World.* London. Bantam Books: a division of Random House. 2002.

Moskowitz, Milton and Levering, Robert and Tkaczyk, Christopher. *The List.* Fortune Magazine. February 8, 2010.

O'Reilly, Terry, and Mike Tennant. *The Age of Persuasion: How Marketing Ate our Culture.* New York: Alfred A. Knopf. 2009.

Pink, Daniel H. *Johnny Bunko: The Last Career Guide You'll Ever Need.* New York: Penguin Group. 2008.

Power, Bill. *China buys the world.* Fortune Magazine. October 26, 2009.

Rubin, Jeff. *Why your world is about to get a whole lot smaller.* New York: Random House Inc. 2009.

Stanley, Thomas J., and William D. Danko. *The Millionaire Next Door.* Marietta Georgia: Longstreet Press Inc. 1996.

Tapscott, Donald. *grown up digital: how the net generation is changing your world.* New York: McGraw-Hill. 2009.

Twenge, Jean. *Generation Me: Why Young Americans Are More Confident, Assertive, Entitled – And More Miserable Than Ever Before.* New York: Free Press. 2006.

Howard J. Breen, has been Chairman and CEO of world-class advertising and integrated agencies in Canada and the USA. A renowned business leader and strategist, he sits on numerous business and charitable boards. His first book, ***A page from a CEO's Diary*** was released in March, 2009. Howard lives in Toronto, Canada with his wife Martha and their two children.

Also by the author

Most adults float through life wondering why they aren't in control of their careers, or future.

Over my 30+ year career in Canada and the States, I have worked with some outrageously exceptional leaders. From them I absorbed invaluable lessons that are captured in *A page from a CEO's Diary.* My hope is that after reading what I've ascertained about business, society, politics, family and love, you'll (re)evaluate your own thinking, values and practices, stop floating in life, and take control of your career and future.